JAILBABY

SUZIE MILLER

CURRENCY PRESS
The performing arts publisher

GRIFFIN
THEATRE
COMPANY

CURRENT THEATRE SERIES

First published in 2023
by Currency Press
Gadigal Land, PO Box 2287 Strawberry Hills, NSW, 2012, Australia
enquiries@currency.com.au
www.currency.com.au

in association with Griffin Theatre Company

Typeset by Brighton Gray for Currency Press.
Printed by Fineline Print + Copy Services, Revesby, NSW.
Cover shows Anthony Yangoyan, photo by Brett Boardman, design by Alphabet.

Currency Press acknowledges the Traditional Owners of the Country on which we live and work. We pay our respects to all Aboriginal and Torres Strait Islander Elders, past and present.

A catalogue record for this book is available from the National Library of Australia

Contents

Jailbaby was first produced by Griffin Theatre Company at the SBW Stables Theatre, Gadigal country, Sydney, on 7 July 2023, with the following cast:

JO RAWLINS / OLIVIA	Lucia Mastrantone
TOM RAWLINS / COACH PETER	Anthony Taufa
AJ / SETH RAWLINS	Anthony Yangoyan

Director, Andrea James
Dramaturg, Declan Greene
Set and Costume Designer, Isabel Hudson
Lighting Designer, Verity Hampson
Composer and Sound Designer, Phil Downing
Stage Manager, Madelaine Osborn
Intimacy and Consent Consultant, Bayley Turner

CHARACTERS

AJ

MRS JO RAWLINS
MR TOM RAWLINS
SETH RAWLINS

(COACH) PETER
COP
CSO
DANI
NURSE
MARNY
OLIVIA
JOHN
SILL
DOCTOR

NOTE ON CASTING

Three actors of no specific gender or age playing numerous roles.

Suggested doubling of AJ and Seth for symbolic purposes, but not a directive.

CONTENT WARNING

This script contains a detailed description of rape. The play also contains descriptions of drug use, suicidal ideation, violence, weapons and homophobic slurs.

This play text went to press before the end of rehearsals and may differ from the play as performed.

SCENE 1

Sound and gesture of snorting coke.

AJ: [*inner voice*] Pumping
Heart crashing against my ribs.

Guys laughing.

I laugh with them.
We finish lines on the dashboard.

Bang it hits me.
To the head, pow.
Xcel laughs at me.

Then
We're out of the car.
Moving over the back fence

I'm keeping up.

Pumping.
Boom boom.
Ribs stretched.

Xcel has a crowbar.
Rams it in.
Cranks the door wide open.

Dragon looks at me
Dunno what he wants?

'My job's to stay out here and keep lookout for the cops, right?'

But no, he flicks his head.
Wants me to follow Xcel.
I get to go IN.

It's dark.
Silent.

Eyes flicking

follow Xcel,
Dragon breathing down my back.

Massive smart TV,
MacBooks,
iPad.

Ka-ching!

One of these alone
Will get me more than the five hundred bucks
to pay for the footy trip

Dragon snarls, he sees two iPhones charging.
Brand new they look.
I'm thinking:
'Who leaves their iPhones at home charging when they go out?'

Xcel slaps me with a couple of big blue IKEA bags.
Then I'm shoving stuff in;
whatever's shiny.

Lots of expensive-looking shit from the shelves
Yes thank you!

It's like stuffing a Christmas stocking—
if you're rich that is!

Then
Socceroos' football jersey. Pristine.
Signed by Tim Cahill!
Fuck me dead!

Draped over the back of a flowery armchair?
I'm putting this baby on,
The guys are taking the motherfucking TV down off the wall.

Xcel growls
'You working, fuckface,
or playing dress-ups?'

Then

An alarm starts up.

Fuck!

Suddenly light on the stairs.
I look at Xcel, look at Dragon.
They look at each other.
Xcel pulls a stocking over his head.
Suddenly he has a fucking knife in his hand,
Dragon nods
He pulls up a stocking over his head too.
Flicks his head at me to get out.

But I'm glued.
Heart.
Pump pump.

My breathing.
Too loud.

MRS R: Seth?

AJ: [*inner voice*] Some old girl.

MRS R: Darling?

AJ: [*inner voice*] Xcel's knife glints

Dragon starts to move the TV
I've got two of the bags.
One on my shoulder, the other dragging on the ground.

Start for the door.

But she's there,
So close.
How'd she—

And the look on her face;
Confusion.

MRS R: Hello?

AJ: [*inner voice*] Then fear.

Xcel bolts.
Thumps me in the back as he

shoves past the woman.
I bump her,
she hits the wall.
Goes down hard,
I lean over, check she's alright.
Xcel yells 'Oi, fuckface!'

Hear myself say 'I'm sorry'.
And then I'm moving.

Big screen gets smashed at the door.
We bolt for the car.

Adrenalin pumping
Coke still running around my body.
Legs moving like the wind.

Hit the car.

'Fuck fuck'

Dragon bangs the dash with his fist.
Xcel can't find the keys.

This jersey's making me sweat big time.

Dragon
yelling
but I don't hear him.

He yells again
'Phones'

Two.

Rip out the SIMs.
Xcel floors it.

Car swerves.

Up a driveway.

Xcel's yelling 'Get rid of him'

'Me?'
'Why?'

'Bitch saw his face.'

Dragon turns to me
'You get caught you say nothing.'

I can't move.

'Wait.'

Then he shoves me out the door.
'You snitch, AJ, and you're dead!
And your mum's dead too. You hear me?'

'Yep yep.'

Dragon lets go of me,
Fall forward.

Then

Sirens

Running
faster than I've ever run in my life.
Legs flying.

Can't look over my shoulder.

Legs burning.

Sirens blaring.

SCENE 2

COP: Description?

MRS R: Tall. Skinny. He had on a football top. Like my son wears.

COP: And he pushed you right?
The one who hurt you?

MRS R: There was a knife.
I thought the big one was going to kill me.
He had a thing over his face but I could see he had writing on his forehead.
A tattoo.

COP: Could you read it?

MRS R: I saw an X, but that's all.
He had a knife.

COP: You see the one who lunged at you?

MRS R: Yes. He was young.
He said 'sorry'.
But one of the older ones had the knife.
Terrifying looking man, big thug.
If my son had come down the stairs / instead of me?

COP: So he admitted liability, the younger one?
He said 'sorry'?

MRS R: Yes, he did.

COP: What else was he wearing?

MRS R: Oh, he had Nikes on. Like my son wears.
Blue and white.

COP: Can you describe his face?

MRS R: Yes. Floppy dark hair. Skinny.
But the other two. Big. Massive. Covered in tattoos.
Faces with a stocking or something. One of them holding the knife; / held it like this …

SETH *enters.*

SETH: Someone had a knife?

MRS R: Oh Seth
It's okay, love …
They've left now, the police are looking after us.
We've lost the laptops and both our iPhones.

SETH: Fuck!

MRS R: Language

SETH: The TV? It's gone, / it was nearly new.

MRS R: I know, love.

Beat as COP *takes in* SETH *then back to business.*

COP: Can you describe the items taken from the shelves?

MRS R: All expensive pieces, I'll go through photos. My husband's coming home, he'll make a full list for insurance purposes. And we'll need a copy of your report.

COP: That's right.

SETH: Great. I won't even be able to watch *Survivor* tonight on the big TV with the surround sound.

MRS R: Darling, that is not the worry right now?

SETH: Everyone else at school will know who got voted off but me!

COP: Mate, your mum was injured!

MRS R: I'm fine, just some bruises.
[*To the* COP *as an aside*] What if they come back?

COP: They'll be miles from here by now!

SETH: Oh NOOOOO.
It was on the chair.
My fucking original jersey /

MRS R: Language, Seth.

SETH *has a full-on meltdown.*

COP *watches him, something weird about this kid.*

SETH: It's fucking gone. I left it here on the chair. It was signed by Tim Cahill.

MRS R: Oh no, not the one Dad got you?—Oh darling, I'm so sorry. [*To* COP] So the jersey the young one was wearing—it must have been my son's. He must have taken it.

SETH: How fucking dare they. It's mine. It's my jersey. I'm going to kill them.

MRS R: Shhh. We'll get you another one, love.

SETH: You can't, it was signed. I fucking want THAT one.

COP: Mate, pipe down, your mum is already shaken up.

SETH: Wait! Did they take MY phone?

He rushes about looking.

MRS R: Do you think I could do the rest of my statement later?

COP: I need it contemporaneously, ma'am.

SETH: My fucking phone!

MRS R: Why don't I meet you down at the station then?

COP: Good. We also need you to do an identikit with our guy down there.

MRS R: I'll just calm him down.

COP *looks at* SETH.

COP: Take it easy, buddy.

SETH: That's MY phone and MY jersey.

COP *exits.*

MRS R: I'm going to make sure the police know how important that jersey is to you.

SETH: I need my phone tomorrow morning!

MRS R: Dad and I'll get one for you first thing.

SETH: Arseholes, why come and take MY stuff.

MRS R: Shhhh. The police will do their best to help us get it back.

SCENE 3

Football (soccer training).

COACH: Move those legs, AJ
This is no dance class, mate
You wanna play professional football?
Or be on stage?

Move it. Yes you, AJ.

You too, Logan.
Both you boys want to come to Queensland, right?
Then no messing about.

Kick it.

Good work, Mohammad.
AJ, get back on your game.

Jesus.

Okay, everyone off.
Not you, AJ.
Two more laps of the field

AJ: What?

COACH: Then come see me.

Okay, boys, gather around.
After your showers head into the clubroom.
Lucas is coming in tonight.
To talk mental strategy.

You hear me,
he's worked with the greats on track and field.
And he's doing this on his own time, and as a favour to me.

So best fucking behaviour, you hear me?
Or the bastard might dump me.

A laugh.

Right.
So for the next three weeks
training will be brutal,
then it's muster for the trip.
Seven a.m. Friday three weeks today, you got it?
Those of you who haven't yet paid your five hundred bucks
won't get on the bus.

AJ *returns, puffing a bit.*

You, over here. Rest of you, well done.

You want to fly up to train with the professionals or not?
You want to blow Maca's mind?

AJ: Yeah.

COACH: So what the fuck are you up to, mate?

AJ: Whaddya mean?

COACH: You're distracted!
Listen to me:
This trip is the chance of a lifetime, Andre.
Maca's the real deal.
He's gonna be looking at YOU.
Show him what you showed me today.
And you're cooked.

AJ: Sorry, Coach.

COACH: We've worked too hard for this.

AJ: I'll be in top nick. Only reason I wouldn't be there is if a truck hit me.

COACH: Well stay away from trucks then, mate!
You hear me?
You want this chance?

AJ: Yeah. More than anything.

COACH: Nothin' bothering you then?

AJ: Nah.

—

COACH: You got the five hundred bucks?

AJ: Working on it.

COACH: You said you'd have it today, mate.

AJ: I was supposed to get paid.

COACH: How much do you have so far?

AJ: Got ripped off, so …

Beat.

COACH: You need a loan?

AJ *cocks his head—really?*

COACH *knows him too well.*

Okay. But it's a loan, you pay me back, son.

AJ: Yeah course.

Beat.

COACH: Right off you go, catch up with the others.

AJ *is happy.*

SCENE 4

MARNY, *AJ's mum's place.*

MARNY: Not lately he don't reside here, no.
That's all I've got to say.

COP: Could he be at his father's residence?

MARNY *laughs.*

MARNY: Yeah, when you find his 'father's residence', you can tell his 'father' that he owes me eighteen years of child support.

COP: So you're telling me if I come back here with a warrant, I won't find anyone out back?

MARNY: I'm not telling you nothing.

COP *leaves.*

Then AJ *appears.*

MARNY *starts shaking, she's anxious.*

Does she light up a cigarette/vape?

Jesus. I don't want the cops over here—what've you done now?

AJ: Nothing.

MARNY: Yeah, so what's with that nice shirt then?

AJ: Coach gave it to me.

MARNY: The gay one?

AJ: So what?

MARNY: You weren't with him Saturday night. I'm not born yesterday, AJ!

He's not going out clubbing with the likes of you on a weekend!

AJ:—

MARNY: Well? Who were you with?

AJ: Some guys.

MARNY: Who?

AJ: Just Xcel and Dragon.

MARNY: AJ?!

MARNY *freaks out. Anxious.*

AJ: We're mates.

MARNY: No you're not.

AJ *turns.*

Those guys are not for you, hon.

AJ: They needed a hand, I was just helping them out

Beat. MARNY *knows exactly what is going on.*

MARNY: Christ, you didn't hurt anyone did you, love?

AJ: Nup.

MARNY: [*gesturing to the shirt*] Just some shoplifting then?

AJ *nods.*

We all want things but we can't always have 'em.

AJ: Yeah well I only got this shirt! The guys have frozen me out of everything else.

AJ's stressed.

MARNY: You okay?

MARNY sighs, opens her arms.

Come here!

He doesn't. She goes to her purse. Takes a twenty and a ten.

For the footy trip? I wish I had more for ya.

AJ pushes her hand with the money away.

AJ: 'S okay. Coach said he'll loan me the five hundred.

MARNY: Well no more shoplifting then, I can't cope with cops coming over.

AJ: I'm fine, Mum.

MARNY: You're eighteen now, that's not juvy anymore.

AJ: Exactly. I'm a man, so get off my case.

MARNY shrugs, AJ leaves.

SCENE 5

Cop shop.

MRS R: Did you manage to retrieve my son's jersey?
He's extremely upset over it.

COP: I noticed.
Here's the deal, Mrs Rawlins; you help us get a conviction and then we help you get as much of your property back as possible.

MRS R: I'm happy to help, those thugs shouldn't be on the streets; carrying knives about.
If my boy had've been the one to disturb them …

COP: Well if you can choose from the line-up, then we put on the pressure to get the names of the others.

MRS R: I'll do my best.

COP: Ready?

MRS R: I'm not sure about seeing their faces again.

She is terrified.

COP: Don't worry, we're starting you easy.

MRS R *nods.*

The line-up occurs.

There's AJ *looking worried.*

MRS R: Oh.
None of the big men are in the line?

COP: Do you recognise *anyone*, Mrs Rawlins?

MRS R: They're all so young.
Not much older than my son.

COP: Yep, the son who wants his jersey back, right?
Do you recognise the man who was wearing that jersey?

MRS R: So young.

COP: Look, ma'am, it's your duty to identify who you can.
You reported this crime, we've done our part, and you've made your insurance claim. So we can't finish our job until you do yours. You understand?

MRS R: But he looked scared when I saw him, it's the other two big guys you need to charge.

COP: Well if you identify him then we ask him for the names of the other two. Bingo. Got 'em.

MRS R: And what happens to him, this kid?

COP: We charge him.

MRS R: Will he get a caution, or something?

COP: Not up to us. If he cooperates, gives us what we want, then things are better for him.

MRS R *looks anxious.*

You don't retrieve anything you lost, until *you* start the ball rolling.

Beat.

You can kiss the jersey goodbye.

Beat.

MRS R: He did say sorry on the night. And he didn't have a knife or anything.

COP: Got it. Which one?

MRS R: Number Three.

COP: Stand forward Number Three.

AJ *steps forward.*

This is the man you saw in your house that night?

MRS R *nods.*

Well done.
Picked him up at McDonald's today. Dumb little prick was still wearing your son's jersey.

MRS R: Oh my god, you have it? The jersey?

COP: In evidence right now.

MRS R: Oh, that's brilliant. Can I take it with me? Seth will be thrilled.

COP: Not yet.
Not till the court case is done.

MRS R: Court?
I don't have to go to court, do I?
I never want to see those two big guys again.

COP: If they plead guilty you don't
But otherwise prosecutors will expect you to show up.
They'll subpoena you!

SCENE 6

Legal interview—cop shop.

AJ: You're legal aid, right?

OLIVIA: [*checking his charge sheet*] Yes. I'm Olivia Marshall.
Look, I'm not going to lie to you—

She looks at his name on the top of the sheet.

Andre,
you're probably looking at jail time.

AJ: I didn't do it. I'm innocent.

OLIVIA: Sure. I'm just giving it to you straight, okay.
You've been charged as part of a serious joint enterprise.
Three of you.
Police have footprints, stolen evidence, and an eyewitness who picked you out from a line-up.

AJ: It wasn't me. It's a mistake.

OLIVIA: Right.
But given the other two haven't been arrested yet, if you wanted to plead guilty ASAP, and give up the names of the co-offenders, then I could do a plea deal with the prosecutors; try to keep you out of jail.

AJ: I'm innocent. I want to plead not guilty.

OLIVIA: A guilty plea at first opportunity is your best bet.
Judges like it when you don't waste the court's time and energy. Andre?

AJ: It's AJ
And I don't want a criminal record.

OLIVIA: I guarantee with a fact sheet like this you'll have a record one way or the other, mate!

AJ: Not if I'm not guilty.

OLIVIA: Okay, well if that's your instructions.

Beat.

They'll keep you here in the police cells for the night now—

AJ: What? All night?

OLIVIA: I'll be back in the morning for the bail hearing.
Sleep on it though, AJ, think over your plea.

AJ: —

OLIVIA: Because if your bail is refused tomorrow, AJ, the risk in jail for you starts as soon as you go to remand.

AJ: I have to get bail, I can't miss football training tomorrow night.

OLIVIA: Listen to me, this is a serious charge—break, enter and steal in company with aggravation … and you were picked up wearing the stolen jersey!

AJ: That was my jersey.

OLIVIA: It's described as one-of-a-kind.

AJ: Tim Cahill signed my jersey too.

OLIVIA: I didn't say it was signed by anyone, mate!

Beat.

Right.

AJ. I'm sending someone in tonight, a guy you need to talk to. He's going to give you some tips to … make it easier inside.

AJ: Why?

OLIVIA: Just so you'll have some intel.
It's helped others …

AJ: —

OLIVIA: You're young and … not so big …

AJ: I can look after myself.

SCENE 7

MRS R *is sitting in the dark with a wine.*

MR R *comes in.*

MR R: What are you doing in the dark?

MRS R: Seth's school called.

MR R: What now?

MRS R: He stole another kid's computer.

MR R *slumps.*

Seth says he didn't mean to take it, that it was an accident.
But … the school found he had tried to sell it on Facebook Marketplace or something.

MR R: Oh Seth!

MRS R: Tom, I had to beg the school not to call the police.

MR R: Oh Jesus.

MRS R: The school said they'd handle it as long as I could prove Seth was seeing a therapist.

MR R: What's wrong with him, we give him everything he wants.
He doesn't need to go around stealing other kids' things.

MRS R: Maybe he wanted the money to replace his football jersey.
He felt terrible about the computer when I spoke to him …

MR R: Yeah, that he got caught! Probably.

MRS R: I've been on the phone all day, I made a donation to the school's building fund. And Holly pulled some strings and got Seth into see this amazing psychiatrist.

MR R: Great. Another one?
How expensive this time?

MRS R: Seth needs to have a report to give the school.

MR R: We've got three reports already. They all say different things. And none of the diagnoses make any difference.

MRS R: I want him retested for autism, and maybe other things.

MR R: Jo. He's just a weird kid. We have to put our foot down now.

MRS R: I want him to have friends.

MR R: He needs to learn his lesson is what he needs. Apply himself, get good grades, shape up. The real worry is not friends, it's about him finding a way to get a job, live independently.

MRS R: The school says he might have to do the HSC over a two-year period now.

MR R: Oh great. More school fees!

MRS R: He's sensitive and he needs understanding. And if he had a real diagnosis—

MR R: Joanne … we're doing all we can, especially you, love.

MRS R: I can't even bear to talk to the other mothers about their children. Their kids are all winning debates and certificates. Going out on dates, working at part-time jobs.

MR R: He's good at maths if he bloody tries. If he ever got off that damn gaming thing. He spends hours and hours in his room on that thing.

MRS R: It's all he has, love. He keeps his feelings inside.

MR R *sighs.*

MR R: I don't know, Jo … I love him, he's our son, but, and this is awful to say, sometimes I just feel … (disappointed).

MRS R *nods.*

MRS R: I'll get him the help he needs. A report would also mean he gets extra marks in the HSC exams with special consideration.

MR R: Good. He needs to do some thinking about the future. He's almost eighteen, for god's sake.

MRS R: I think he's worse, more sensitive, since we were robbed? Don't you?

MR R *shrugs.*

MR R: He's the same, Jo.

MRS R: No. This wouldn't have happened if we weren't robbed. I know it.

I'm having nightmares about it myself; I don't want to go to court, Tom.

MR R: But you want the insurance payout?

MRS R: Of course.

MR R: Well then we need to cooperate with the police.

SCENE 8

AJ *takes up the phone to talk.*

JOHN: AJ?

AJ *nods.*

Name's John. Jonno.
Your lawyer, Olivia Marshall, sent me.

AJ: Hey.

JOHN: You gotcha yourself into some shit, hey, mate?

AJ: Yeah.

JOHN: Hear you've got a bail hearing tomorrow?

AJ: In the morning, gotta get out of here for footy training tomorrow night.

JOHN: AFL?

AJ: Nah, soccer.

JOHN: League's my game.
Sharks boy through and through.
You follow rugby?

AJ: Ah yeah. Tigers a bit.

JOHN: Ah they're rough bastards!

Awkward silence.

JOHN *stares at* AJ *through the glass*

AJ*'s eyes are everywhere.*

You got a girl?

AJ: Yeah. On and off. Dani.

JOHN: Good, good.

Awkward silence.

Your lawyer wants me to give you some tips.

AJ: Are you a social worker or something?

JOHN: Fuck, do I look like social, mate?
I'm ex-con. Spent twenty-five inside for murder.

AJ: Fuck.

JOHN: Look, if you go into the jail system here's a few things you need to know straight up.
First thing—make sure someone puts money in buy-up.
You need cash in there to buy smokes, which you can trade for other shit.
Also you'll eat better if you have cash in buy-up.

AJ: Yeah, I'm getting bail tomorrow so I won't—

JOHN *slams his hand down, gets* AJ*'s attention.*

JOHN: Second, you won't fit into any groups. You're not part of any gang.
You got no protection, buddy.
Not in remand.
And not in the big jail if you go down.

AJ: I'm okay.

JOHN: [*intensely now, shake* AJ *up*] Thing is no-one wants to hear this
So I'll make it quick.
This ain't going away, kid.
Inside, you are going to get a lot of 'attention'.

With that face and that look about you—you're fucking done for.
But I'm about to give you a road map.

AJ: Don't fucking need it, man.

JOHN *puts his foot down.*

JOHN: Oi mate!
The risk for you starts in remand!
And then in the big house you look out for the ones who have long sentences.
You hear me?
They're the ones who have nothing else to lose.

AJ: —

JOHN: They're all about power.
So they need to fuck up the weaker ones.

AJ *laughs awkwardly.*

AJ: Nah. Not me.

JOHN: Yeah well maybe not you then, kid.
But—
Doesn't mean you're gay or nothing,
Inside the rules are different.

AJ: I said I gotta girl.

JOHN: Exactly.
So try to think of her …
when they ram their cocks in your mouth …

AJ: No fucking way!

JOHN: [*calm, matter-of-fact*] You have to relax your throat because you need to not choke to death.
Breathe through your nose.

No shame. It's about survival.

Big tip:
Try not to think about it.
Even if they call you a girl, you're no fucking pussy.
You've got a chick on this side, think of her.

AJ *takes the phone from his ear.*

JOHN *does one big slam of the glass, that makes* AJ *pick it up again.*

You listen to this.
You might not need it, but you'll be glad if you do.
If they start to fuck you up the arse and you try and hold back, it will rip through your fucking arsehole, you hear me?

AJ: Jesus.

JOHN: But these are tough motherfuckers so they have to fuck you up rather than make it gentle.
Can't look like pooftas.

AJ: Fuck!!

JOHN: Shut up and listen.

Best deal is to try and relax and push back on it, don't try to resist.
It'll be brutal until you agree to be someone's boy.
Choose quickly if you can.
If you have to.

AJ: Nah.
You're just fucking with me.

JOHN: Yeah because I got nothing else to do with my evenings!
It's about survival in there, mate.
You probably don't know this, but when someone fucks you up the arse, and your prostate is pushed on, there's a chance you get a stiffy.
Doesn't make you gay.

Unless—

AJ: I'm not fucking gay.

JOHN: Just as well, the gay kids get it so much worse in there.

AJ *takes the phone away from his ear.*

JOHN *bangs on the window glass.*

AJ *puts the phone back to his ear.*

You need to hear this.

AJ: Are you getting off on this, or something, bro?

JOHN: [*menacing*] You fucking watch yourself, Andre.

Brings his voice back.

Look, mate, when you're back out on the outside no-one will know.

Promise you.

No-one will ever speak of it.

Yeah?

AJ: Why are you telling me this bullshit?

JOHN: I was just like you when I first went in.
Skinny.
Long time ago now.

I got fucked up pretty badly.

Don't like talking about this shit, kid.
But I'm paying my dues because, yeah

I've been on both ends of it.

Not proud of that. I admit.

AJ: Fuck off
I play football
I can hold my own.

AJ *slams down phone and bashes on glass (and screams) to get the hell out of there.*

SCENE 9

Psychiatrist session.

DOCTOR: Anything you tell me in here is privileged.

SETH: Right.

DOCTOR: Can you tell me more about how you feel like an outsider?

SETH: Only at home. And at school.

DOCTOR: Has something happened to make you feel that way?

SETH: You mean was there kiddy-fiddling or something?

DOCTOR: Well, no, just anything that … but …

SETH: I'm just not like other kids and people don't like it.

DOCTOR: You're, what, seventeen; all teens feel like outsiders.

SETH: Yeah yeah yeah.

DOCTOR: Is there anywhere you don't feel like an outsider?

SETH: Online.

DOCTOR: So do you consider your online community your friends?

SETH: Look. I'm just here because of my parents … they want me to be … something else.

DOCTOR: Like what, Seth?

SETH: Like other kids.

DOCTOR: And what is that?

SETH: Talk about going to uni, have girlfriends, go out.

DOCTOR: Why do you think your parents want you to be doing those things?

SETH: It makes them feel better. Successful.

DOCTOR: Why do you think that is the case?

SETH: Ask them.

DOCTOR: I'm asking you?

SETH: So I'm here because I guess you're supposed to make me normal.

DOCTOR: Your mother thinks the home invasion has made you more fearful, more emotional.

SETH: Good.

DOCTOR: Good?

SETH: Gives her a reason to explain why I do things.

DOCTOR: I don't understand.

SETH *rolls his eyes.*

Beat.

Can you tell me why you stole the computer at school, Seth?

SETH: I wanted to.

DOCTOR: Then why try to sell it?

SETH: I need the money.

DOCTOR: What for?

SETH: To make a future.

DOCTOR: What kind of future?

SETH *shrugs.*

Can you share it with me?

SETH: Yeah right!

DOCTOR: What does that mean, Seth?

SETH: They're paying you, aren't they?

DOCTOR: Your parents?

SETH: Yeah, they're paying you, so whose side are you on?

DOCTOR: Are there sides?

SETH: —

DOCTOR: What will make you happy, Seth?

SETH: Not having to pretend all the time.
Just being me.

Beat.

DOCTOR: Perhaps I could help you find a way to enjoy the things that you want to do, and do some other things that make your parents happy? Would that work, Seth? Like a win-win situation?

SETH: You tell me, you're the doctor.
You're the one getting paid here!

DOCTOR: Can you tell me what you love to do the most?

SETH: Be alone, play Switch.

DOCTOR: Could you do that and also get good grades?
Make some friends?
That way you're happy and your parents are too.

SETH: Yeah.
Look, you can take credit for this if you want.
I've made a friend.
An offline friend.
This guy at school.
Sebastian. I call him Bash.

DOCTOR: And what do you and Sebastian do together?

SETH: He said I could sit with him at lunch.

DOCTOR: Do you enjoy that?

SETH: Not really. But when I tell Mum she's happy.
She even gives me all this money to buy things.

DOCTOR: And how do you feel about having a friend?

SETH: It means my parents don't hassle me.

DOCTOR: Do you have any joy at talking to Sebastian?

SETH *shrugs.*

Do you get annoyed with him, like you do with some of the other kids?

SETH: No.

DOCTOR: Why not?

SETH: He doesn't say much; just lets me use my Switch.

DOCTOR: That sounds like a thoughtful friendship.

SETH: My parents can talk about it.

DOCTOR: They can talk about … ?

SETH: To their friends. They can feel like normal parents.
And you can take the credit if you want.
That's a win-win.
Isn't it?

SCENE 10

OLIVIA *arrives at the police cell to talk to* AJ.

AJ *stands, the pants she gave him to put on are too big around the waist and falling down.*

AJ *folds the pants around the waist so they won't fall down.*

AJ: Thanks for the gear,
But the fucking pants are too big round the waist.
Can I use this as a belt?

AJ *is holding the tie. She takes it from him.*

OLIVIA: No. And you look great, AJ.

She starts to put the tie on around his neck. AJ *stands there like a child going to school. Their eyes meet.* OLIVIA *stops then continues tying.*

Shirt fits.

AJ: You said it was a small men's
But it can't be.
Wrong label I reckon.

OLIVIA *smiles.*

Cops want me sitting in a cell, where they can see me.
Don't want me hanging myself with the tie, they reckon.

I'm not a fucking emo.

OLIVIA *smiles, he's funny. Then she is professional.*

OLIVIA: Who's coming today to speak for you?

AJ *shakes his head—no-one.*

You have a social worker?

AJ: Nup.

OLIVIA: We need someone to vouch for you. Tell us what a good character you have. So the courts don't think you're going to cause havoc if they give you bail. We need someone to prove links to the community to show you are not a flight risk. Any teachers from school?

AJ: No way.

OLIVIA: Priest? A rabbi?

AJ *laughs.*

Any adults you get along with?

AJ *shakes his head.*

Your mum coming?

AJ *keeps shaking his head.*

Shall I call her?

AJ: No. She doesn't like going to court.

OLIVIA: Jesus, mate, can you give me anything at all? You have any hobbies?
Sport? Didn't you say you played rugby or something yesterday?

AJ: Soccer.

OLIVIA: You have a coach?

AJ: Peter.

OLIVIA: Would he come to court?

AJ: Nah. Don't want him knowing I'm in trouble.

OLIVIA: I'll grab your phone from the police and try some numbers.
You've got a much better chance of bail with a few good references.

AJ: I dunno anyone.

OLIVIA: Okay well I'll see what I can come up with.
See you in there, okay?
[*To* POLICE OFFICER] I'm done thanks.

POLICE OFFICER *leads* OLIVIA *away.*

AJ: [*inner voice*] Big cop arrives, gun on his waist.
Tells me 'your turn'.

Leads me to court.

Wait a bit.
Wait a bit more.

Go in.

Sit in the wooden box.
Look around.
Judge stares at me.
Asks my name.

[*To* JUDGE] Andre Jackson.

[*Inner voice*] See Olivia looking serious at the big table.
She's standing up.
Microphone in front of her.

Papers are moved around.
Someone's talking.
Olivia is up then sits.
Then up again.

Then down.

Someone comes up to another wooden box,
there's a microphone there too.

It's Coach Peter.
There he is.
Oh shit
I told Olivia not to call him
He's gonna give me hell at training tonight.
He's gonna trash me something shocking for it
Make me run more laps of the field.
Fuck it.

AJ *looks at* COACH, *but* COACH *is looking at* OLIVIA.

Can't believe he showed up.
He came to court.
To speak up for me.
He's gonna get me out of here.

The big man looks small in here.

Someone comes up and Coach Peter holds his hand in the air.
He looks at the judge
Says something.

I look at all the people in the audience.
All these strangers.
Like they're watching a movie or something
A little kid on his mum's knee starts crying.
She's trying to make him quiet down.

Couple of big bros sitting at the back
Stand up a bit taller
Don't want to look freaked out
But I am a bit

And then Coach is talking.
Except Olivia keeps calling him Mr Scanlon.

OLIVIA: Mr Scanlon, can you please tell the court what your occupation is?

COACH: I'm a soccer coach for the Bears, and I also assist coaches who scout for pro-league players.

OLIVIA: And, Mr Scanlon, can you tell the court how you know the accused?

COACH: Andre Jarrah is known to me as AJ. He is an outstanding young player, one with immense potential. I was shaping him to play for state and then hoping for nationals. He's a good kid, always helps out around the club. He's a fun-loving and nice lad.

AJ *likes this.*

OLIVIA: Can you tell us something of your experience of Andre's homelife.

COACH: AJ has done it tough in life.
His father was violent and left the family when Andre was very young.

AJ *doesn't like this so much looks down.*

I support many young men in crisis.
Try to work as a role model.

AJ: [*inner voice*] Jesus, he's going to make everyone think I'm a pussy or something.
Fucking hell.
Everyone looking at me like I'm a loser.
Thanks, Coach
Thanks a lot.

COACH: AJ has an extraordinary soccer skillset. I have never seen anything like it. A natural talent. The first time he came to the club, he was only a boy of about eight, no football boots, nothing. But he kicked that ball, and the way he kicked it—I was there with a few guys from my pro days, and this kid was the real deal. A champion raw-talent striker right there before us. I've been training him ever since. He's a natural with a proper skillset now.

AJ: [*inner voice*] Look around
Hope someone I know
hears Coach Peter talk like this.
Calling me a 'natural', for real.

COACH: AJ is to go on a football trip in a few weeks, and the trip is going to be the beginning of everything for him. There are a few football talent scouts going, and there is no doubt that he will most certainly be spotted.

AJ: [*inner voice*] I love that everyone can hear this.
I'm gonna be famous, a top player
I'll sign people's jerseys myself. Make them valuable.

COACH: It's a proper start for a young man.
I'm quite sure AJ could be chosen.
With his capacity he has an opportunity that many do not.
His family life will never offer him something like this. A future like this.

His mother struggles with addiction issues and AJ has not been parented appropriately.

AJ: [*inner voice*] Hang on.
Don't say that.
She's done her best.
And she's clean at the moment.
Coach's never met her.
Thank god she didn't come.
Breathe out.

COACH: I believe in Andre, he can get there, he needs bail and a clean record to be able to exercise this possibility.
He can't have a criminal record if he is to play elite sport.

AJ *is thinking things are going really well.*

AJ: [*inner voice*] I think the judge is impressed or he fucking should be.

COACH *steps down and goes to leave.*

He turns to AJ *and nods.*

AJ *nods back to him too.*

Weird
We've never nodded to each other before.

Olivia sits down at that table.
What's happening?
Judge talking.
Don't understand.
Olivia nodding, writing stuff down.
Judge still talking.
Not looking at me, everyone is super-quiet.

When I get to training tonight
I'll tell all the boys I had a close one.

Judge is looking at papers,
Talking about how terrified the family we robbed was.
I think about the lady on the stairs that came down.
All that fear on her face

Feel bad.
She looked real scared.

Then I hear him
Judge says
'Refused.'
'Bail refused.'
But he's just—
What?
Why?
Grit my teeth, don't let tears come out.

Gotta get to training tonight.
Olivia stands up
Talking about another person,
Another name
Benji

Look at all the people in the court.
A lady makes a sad face and stares at me.
Dudes at the back are checking me out.
What's going on?
What happens now?

A cop leads me out of the box.
I look back.

[*To* GUARD] Where are you taking me?

SCENE 11

OLIVIA: [*officious, in a rush*] Bail was refused, AJ. There's a hearing date set for September.

AJ: What? You said I'd get bail.

OLIVIA: I said I would try.

AJ: But Coach Peter …

OLIVIA: He was great.
But sadly not enough.

I told you, it's a serious crime, AJ.
They'll be taking you into the remand centre at the end of the / day.

AJ: I didn't do anything.

OLIVIA: Right.

AJ: I was gonna be lookout.
Just needed the money for my football trip, that's all.

OLIVIA: Put my number on your contact list, you can make a legal call to me if you want to change your plea. I'll try to see you into the remand centre when the police brief comes out.

And …
remember your chat with John.

AJ: Hey, don't just leave me here.

Beat.

OLIVIA: Sorry, AJ, I can't do anymore today.

Can you change out of those clothes and give them to the officer.
I have to get them cleaned for my next client.

AJ *is taken away by* POLICE.

SCENE 12

SETH: There's a new Mario-and-Zelda-themed Nintendo store opening in Tokyo.
I want to be there so badly!

DOCTOR: Sounds interesting.

SETH: Yes and I have exciting news. Thanks to you!
Last time I was here, you inspired me,
because you said I could have my own plans and also keep my parents happy.

DOCTOR: I'm glad you took it to heart, Seth.

SETH: And this Japanese store has every piece of *Mario Cart* merch
Luigi, Princess Peach, even the obscure ones, like Toad, Wa-Luigi, Yoshi, Toadette, Diddy Kong, and Wario.

I’ve done more than eight hundred hours of *Zelda* and *Mario World.*
And I spoke to them, they like people who speak English.
I’m good with English.
Speaking it and stuff.

DOCTOR: What, you called them?

SETH: Did a video chat with them.

And got on Duolingo
so I can learn a bit of Japanese too.
Konichiwa
Ogenki desu ka?
Get this
I’m going to go and live in Tokyo forever.

DOCTOR: What? Living there? In Japan?

SETH: Finally be in a place where I can be me.
I’ve secretly been saving for the airfare.

DOCTOR: Can we just break this down a bit?

SETH: The store put an ad on their website
Saying they wanted English speakers for the store
Hiring a bunch of them
SO
I had a Zoom interview.

And get this
I got a job!

DOCTOR: Wait a minute
Let’s just back up a bit.
I thought you were saving for—
I thought the dream was just to *visit* the store one day?

SETH: Not anymore.
Cos of you I’m dreaming big.

You said I could plan my own life
and so I thought about it
and now—

I reckon you're right
I can live and work in Japan by myself.

DOCTOR: One day, maybe.
But for now I'd—
I'd say it's great to have a dream, Seth.
But I'm worried—
What do your parents think?

SETH: Oh I'm not telling them.
They know nothing.
And remember, you can't tell them.
Besides, you'd get all the blame.
It was all your idea!

DOCTOR: Seth, I think I said you needed to think of a plan to do things that make you happy and other things that make your parents happy.
Remember?

SETH: Yep
But they want me to go straight to uni.

DOCTOR: Well can't you visit the store in Tokyo over summer and then—

SETH: To go to uni
I have to get great grades in maths
I have to.

DOCTOR: But I saw your last report
you've got great maths grades, don't you?

SETH: They're slipping.
Mum and Dad don't know.

They think all the talking to you is helping.
And it is.
It's just …
when I took Ritalin last year my maths grades were so much better,

But I stopped taking the Ritalin
and now my grades are …

DOCTOR: Why did you stop taking the Ritalin?

SETH: Lost the prescription and …
I guess if I don't get the marks, then I have no choice but to take the job in Japan and drop the idea of uni

DOCTOR: Do you need a prescription?

SETH: That's a great idea. Yeah I reckon that'll fix me.

SCENE 13

Silverwater Remand Centre.
Green outfit that AJ *puts on.*

AJ: [*inner voice*] Fuck
I'm butt naked.
'Spread your bum cheeks'
Screws gazing in my cake hole
'Turn around'
'Lift your ball sack'
Jesus

One of them throws me the greens
Top has a stain on it.
Put them on.
Follow the screw.

Grey walls
blue floor
Massive fluoro flickers.
Cells.
One after the other
Mad banging and shouting.
Screw stops at a door …
A body lurches at the perspex.
Slam!
Heart pumping.

But the screw laughs and opens the next cell.

'Here's your five-star suite, kid'
Same size as Mum's bathroom at home
Without the broken pink tiles
Just a sink and a silver shitter. Gross. Stinks.
But only one bed
So I gotta fucking
private room!
Yes.

He laughs.

That fucking guy John scared me shitless for no reason.

Lie on the bed.
Grey blanket.

Got no buy up.
No phone calls.
No-one visits.
Nothing.
Can't stop thinking …
shit things
Over and over in my mind.
Just here on my own
all these days,
and it does my head in.

Try to remember 'I'm getting out soon.'
Gotta get out of here. Gotta get out.
Gotta get on the football trip.

Talk to Mum out loud
Tell her about my day.

And Dani,
tell her the funny stories, and some scary ones.
And about all the drugs they smuggle in here!
Swear at her at other times cos she fucking doesn't come to visit.

Over the loudspeaker
a voice calls my MIN number.

Fuck
A visitor?
Or—?

Screw I report to
tells me ‘it’s your girlfriend’
Oh Dani!
Thank you.

Walk fast.
Heart happy.

But,
I see
he’s fucking bullshitting me.

SCENE 14

Visitors’ room with OLIVIA.

OLIVIA *has a stack of manila folders with different names on them.*

They each have pink legal ribbon around them with different male names on them.

When AJ *sits she fossicks through the pile and brings up his file.*

OLIVIA: Andre
I’ve seen the full police brief.
It’s definitely lengthy—

AJ: I have to get out of here
I’ve got the football trip.
I’ve already missed heaps of training
My coach is gonna be real pissed off.

OLIVIA: Police case is strong, AJ.
If you change to a guilty plea
we’ll try to make a deal; see if we can get you out.

AJ: But if I plead guilty I’ll get a record?

Beat.

OLIVIA: Look, AJ,

They have your fingerprints, your DNA, the football jersey
and an eyewitness that puts you at the scene.
So I'd say you're going to get a record no matter what happens.

AJ: Even if I was just getting paid to be lookout?

OLIVIA *sighs, she's going to tell him for the last time.*

OLIVIA: Makes no difference.
A serious crime was committed,
and someone got hurt.
And, AJ,
it doesn't matter who pushed her
or how much you're 'sorry'
It's not going to make you not guilty.

AJ: You reckon if I plead guilty can I get out in time to go to my football trip?

OLIVIA: I told you if you gave evidence against your co-offenders
then maybe I could keep you out of prison.
I can't promise anything; you should have done it at the bail hearing …
But I could still try and do a deal.
You'd have to enter a guilty plea and make a statement giving names and descriptions of the guys you were with at the robbery. No tricks.

AJ: And I could get out?

OLIVIA: Maybe.
Shall I change your plea to guilty?
Put the prosecutors on notice that you can offer some information, and that I'm looking for no jail time?

AJ: You think I should?

OLIVIA: Yes.

AJ: Okay. I'll plead guilty and you talk to the prosecutors.

OLIVIA: Done.

AJ: Can you get my mum to come in to see me?
You have her number on the file.

OLIVIA *looks at him.*

Please.

OLIVIA *digs into another file.*

OLIVIA: Here's a phone card with a few dollars' credit.
We only give out one per client though.
But you call her and tell her yourself.

AJ: Thanks.
When you talk to the prosecutor, will they get the guys off the streets so they can't get at me?

OLIVIA: Let's try for that, shall we? It'll be on video link. You won't even have to sit in court. It'll be quick.

AJ: Yep.
I just want to get out fast.
I'm always looking over my shoulder in here.
Got no mates or anything.
Nothin'.

SCENE 15

AJ: [*inner voice*] Line up for the phone for fifty minutes.
Try and call Mum
Three times
Keep going to voicemail.

Don't leave messages because I'll just waste the credit.
A huge fella's watching me
Pressuring me to hurry

Try Dani instead.
She picks up
My heart soars.

[*Into phone*] Dani, it's me.

DANI: Cockhead!
Where the fuck are you?

AJ: Do you know if my mum is okay?

DANI: No idea.
Ask her yourself?

AJ: I'm in remand.

DANI: You're in jail, for real?

AJ: Nah nah just remand
Come visit me?
It's just a train to Parra …
I fucking miss you, Dan.

DANI: You owe me a big apology.

AJ: I know I know
And I apologise—

DANI: Yeah well
I've been through this shit before, AJ.
You keep breaking my heart.
I gotta go, gotta get to work.

AJ: Babe, I'm gonna make it up to you big time.

DANI: Really?
How are you gonna make it up to me while you're in jail?

AJ: I'm getting out soon.
Cooperating.
I promise if you come in and see me soon
and
we'll make plans.

DANI: Why'd you have to go and sleep with that bitch?

AJ: Oww, baby.
I'm a fucking dickhead.

DANI: Fucked me up big time, AJ
I cried for weeks.

AJ: Oh, bunny
I'm so sorry.
I'll be out of here soon

Getting this whole shitshow fixed up soon.
Doing it on some screen inside here to make it fast.

Beat.

But you gotta come out and see me before I leave.

DANI: I'm a bit scared to go into a jail.

AJ: Babe
Please. It's just remand.

DANI: I don't know, AJ.

AJ: Please
I miss you so much
I miss your smile and stuff
How you push yourself up close to me.
Wearing your shirt skirt
and your perfume
I love the smell of it
Reminds me of …
Being a kid.

Weird.
Come on, baby
When I get out
let's start again.
Get my mum and we can all go to Queensland and live.

DANI: Your mum!

AJ: Don't want to leave her behind.
Get in any trouble.

DANI: Right.

AJ: Dani,
I've never told you this
But
I think you are the love of my life.

[*Inner voice*]And as I say this I think I mean it.
I think maybe she is.

[*Into phone*] I want to move in together
Be with you forever, Dani?
What do you say?

DANI: Fuck!
You serious?

AJ: I'm going to get out of here
And play professionally.
Coach Peter really believes in me.
And you can be my WAG. My one and only WAG.

DANI *laughs*

I'm pleading guilty and
coming home
I miss you, Dani.

He gets emotional.

My bunny, my girl.
My WAG!

DANI: I miss you too.
Cockhead!

AJ *laughs.*

AJ: Oh babe.
Hand on heart I'm never cheating on you again.
Search up great places in Queensland
then come in and tell me
And bring photos of / you in your undies …

VOICEOVER: This phone call has reached its limit and has been terminated.

AJ: [*inner voice*] Fuck. Time's up.
Guy behind me muscles in
Give him the phone

Go back to my cell
Alone.
Lie under the grey blanket,

Pull out my cock and imagine Dani's mouth on it.
Sucking the guts out of it.
When I come I imagine her with me, moaning.

SCENE 16

A guy approaches AJ *and heavies him off to one side.*

AJ: What the fuck, man?

GUY: Shut your fucking gob, kid.

AJ: Who are you? What do you want?

GUY *laughs hideously.*

Hey. I'm not like that.

GUY: Like what, poofta?

AJ: Nothing. But I'm straight, okay.

GUY: What're you fucking calling me?

AJ: Nothing. Hey, man. I'm just—

GUY: You AJ?

AJ *nods.*

Got a message for you.

AJ *is frozen.* GUY *bashes him over the head.*

You got ears?

AJ *nods.*

AJ: Yep. You've got a message for me.

GUY: Do you know who from.

AJ *shakes his head.*

You love your mum, fuckface?

AJ *freezes, gets another thump over the head.*

AJ: Yes of course I fucking do.

GUY: You wanna see her face bleeding out on the side of the road with a knife to her guts?

AJ *shakes his head. Scared.*

Who knows what else'll be done to her before then even.

AJ: What the fuck! What is this?

GUY: Dragon and Xcel your bros?

AJ *freezes, nods a little.*

They have a message for you.

Your mama lives at thirty-five Beatty Street, right?

AJ: —

GUY: She'll be gagging for them to kill her.
Think of your mama, kid.

AJ: No. Tell them no.

GUY: You dog them out and your mum that gets it. You hear me?

AJ *nods.*

AJ: I haven't done anything.

GUY: And you won't, right?

AJ: Of course not.

GUY: I got my eye on you, fuckface.
You say nothing about those bros ever, you hear?

AJ: Yep.

GUY: You're pleading guilty, kid.
You're pleading guilty and taking the fall.

AJ *nods.*

GUY *hits him over the head again.*

Can't hear you.

AJ: Yes. Yes. I'm not saying anything. Taking the fall.

GUY *pushes him away as he walks off.*

SCENE 17

The court is displayed on a tiny square on a computer screen which AJ *can barely see—he is so outside the process. In court it is on a television screen.*

AJ: Olivia?
Ms Marshall.

OLIVIA: AJ.
Hi there.
How are you?
We have a reasonably decent prosecutor.

AJ: This is a real court, yeah?

OLIVIA: Yep, I'm in the courtroom.
So's everyone else, and you're up there on the screen.

AJ: But I don't have your pants and shirt and tie to wear.

OLIVIA: Lucky you look good in prison greens then.

AJ: I can hardly see everyone.

OLIVIA: Well there's not many here you'd know anyway, AJ. But your mum's here up the back.

AJ: She is, my mum is there?
Is she okay?

OLIVIA: She seems okay.

AJ: Are you sure? I can't see her.

OLIVIA: Yep.

AJ: Is my coach there?

OLIVIA: No, he couldn't make it today.
He's said he's preparing for the football trip.
Said you'd know what he meant.

AJ: Yeah. I'm going on that.

OLIVIA: I have to be quick, AJ, there's a few others on the list for me to attend to today.
This is what will happen:
You will state your full name and enter your plea.
That means you will say
GUILTY when they ask you how you plead.

I told the prosecution you are providing evidence against your co-offenders.

AJ: Yeah. Nah, I'm not doing that.

OLIVIA: What?
Have you changed your mind?

AJ: Yeah.

OLIVIA: Why? Did someone threaten you?
Because they're bluffing you.
That's how it works.

AJ: Nup, I don't think so—

OLIVIA: I'll make submissions to the prosecution that you'll need police protection.

AJ: Yeah like the cops are gonna protect me and my / mum

OLIVIA: Thought you wanted to get out of here
Go to your football camp?

AJ: I fucking do!

OLIVIA: Your coach is getting everything ready.

AJ: Please, just get me out without me having to name the others.

OLIVIA*'s last try.*

OLIVIA: AJ. It's now or never. You don't get another chance at this after today.
You're being sentenced.

AJ: [*inner voice*] I picture my mum.

Fear on her face
She doesn't deserve this.

Makes me think of the woman at the house we robbed
Fear on her face too
Feel bad.

[*To* OLIVIA] What will I get?

OLIVIA: If you don't cooperate and give evidence then you're looking at two to six years on the top.
So all in all, likely one to four years on the bottom.

AJ: [*inner voice*] I pretend I know what she is talking about.
I could do one year maybe. I've already done a month.
At least I won't stay at this place
They'll have to take me some place else.

There's no air-conditioning in the waiting room here.

OLIVIA: AJ?

AJ: [*to* OLIVIA] Yes.

OLIVIA: I'm urging you.
Give the names to the police.
It's now or never.

AJ: [*inner voice*] Now or never.
Fuck.
[*To* OLIVIA] NO. I can't.

OLIVIA: Right.
Can you see the judge on the video?

AJ: I can hardly see anything.

OLIVIA: Okay. Stand by, AJ.

> AJ *is suddenly quiet. Just him and a video camera and screen. The court looks so far away.*

AJ: [*inner voice*] Someone asks him what I plead.

> *He looks for* OLIVIA*'s face but can't see it. No-one is talking.*

Then there she is.

OLIVIA: Andre, please could you talk into the microphone in front of you and state what your plea is.

AJ: Guilty.

OLIVIA: Your Honour, my client has entered his plea of guilty and further to that I propose submissions in mitigation. He is only eighteen years old, was raised in government housing by his single mother, who is here today.

I tender a reference by Mr Peter Scanlon, referred to and listed in the appendix as Document A. This document attends to Andre's skill in football and his significant potential to play at an elite level. If Andre goes to prison today he will not be able to play for a professional team. The consequences of this are dire for my client. The only qualifications he has to get ahead in life centre upon this opportunity.

AJ *hangs his head. This is everything just gone.*

My client is under no illusion that he will not be incarcerated, but I urge Your Honour to consider the significant loss of his football career as punishment already to be endured by Andre. I particularly and respectfully urge Your Honour when sentencing, to also take into account my client's tender age, his small frame and youthful boyish looks. This does not bode well for him in prison, and there is every possibility he will have a more challenging incarceration period than men of greater stature and age. I ask respectfully that Your Honour consider this and settle on a prison sentence that is toward the lower end of the scale.

AJ: [*inner voice*] Fuck is she's talking about—
Jesus, why is she saying this bullshit?

He looks down.

Stop listening.

And then it's over.
Just her and me.

OLIVIA: It went well.

AJ: Really? I get out?

OLIVIA: Three years on the top and two on the bottom.

AJ: What the fuck does that mean?
Two years.
And football …
I'll be twenty years old.
That's like old, so old.

I don't want to miss two years of football.
I can't.

I want to see my teammates, my coach.
I can't do this.

I need to play.
Do you understand?

—

Okay, okay, I will give up the other names.
I'll do it.
I can't stay here.
I can't face it.
I'll tell the police everything.
I want to get out.

OLIVIA: It's too late, AJ.

Screen flickers off.

AJ: Ms Marshall?

A CSO *comes and cuffs* AJ.

The guy is rough, cuffs too tight.

You gotta loosen them.
They're way too tight.

CSO *ignores him.*

AJ *kicks the side of the room.*

He's in a blind panic.

CSO *shoves* AJ *who fights back.*

I can't feel my fucking wrists.

CSO *lifts his baton, leans all his weight onto* AJ.

AJ *sees his own face in a reflection.*

SCENE 18

MR R *returns home.* MRS R *is hysterical.*

MR R: I'm here, Jo. Please tell me: what's going on?

MRS R: Tom, I haven't stopped crying.

MR R: Is Seth okay?

MRS R: The school called.
He's been selling Ritalin to the students at school.

MR R: What?

MRS R: I think he's trying to make friends.

MR R: Are you out of your mind?
That's drug-dealing, Joanne!
Are the police involved?

MRS R: I've been hysterical.
Seth! It's our Seth!

MR R: Jo—has he been arrested?

MRS R: Oh god. Don't say that. You're freaking me out.

MR R: Jo! ARE THE POLICE INVOLVED?

MRS R: No the school didn't call the police. The school doesn't want any media attention, thank god. Sarah came down with me to the school—of course her Harry is head boy so it made me feel like a complete failure. Seth and drugs. Tom, what are we going to do?

MR R: We have to be super-tough. This is criminal, he's a criminal now.

MRS R: Don't talk like this, Tom. He's having therapy. You're scaring me.

MR R: Cancel that doctor, I'll call Roger, he's a barrister, I'll get advice in case Seth has to talk to the police … Go through the med cabinet now, dispose of everything. Every headache pill, every pain reliever. SETH. SETH, come here now.

SETH *appears, he has his Switch under his arm. His father sees it.* MRS R *is crying.*

MR R: What were you thinking? You want to go to jail like some no-hoper? Is that it?

SETH: No.

MRS R: Stop it, Tom, this is not the way we talk to our son.

MR R: What have you got to say for yourself?

SETH: Nothing.

MRS R: He's sorry.

SETH: I'm sorry.

MR R: Who gave you the extra Ritalin—this new bloody psych?

SETH: Yeah. He thought I needed more, but when I realised I didn't, I just shared them …

MRS R: It's all / a mistake.

MR R: Well that's most certainly the end of him then. There are going to be huge consequences, Seth. HUGE. Firstly, we monitor all your meds from now on, you can't have any personal responsibility on that anymore. You can't be trusted.

MRS R *is crying.*

Secondly, no more time in your room—and hand over that thing.

SETH *clutches his Switch.*

SETH: What?

MR R: Consequences, Seth. That's the only way people learn how to do the right thing. Give it to me.

SETH: No.

MR R *snatches it from him.*

No. It's mine.

MR R: Give it to me.

SETH: It's mine.

MR R: I paid for the damn thing.

There's a struggle. MR R *has it.*

MR R: You don't get it back until you can behave yourself.
I want great maths marks and you'll stay out of your room from now on.

A transition.

A new world.

New jail.

Bigger, more intimidating.

More isolated.

SCENE 19

AJ *arrives today at big jail.*

AJ: [*inner voice*] Get cuffed when I fall out of the truck.

I see barbed wire everywhere.

Look up at the sky,
Blue,
then the screws shove me inside.

This is it:
Proper jail.

I get searched.
Yelled at by the screws.
I'm not fast enough.

This place is older.
Dingy.

Crowded here,
three to a cell.
Two big guys in with me.
Don't talk to me.
One's bald but that could just be cos his head is shaved;
Too scared to stare and get a proper look to figure it out.
Other one is massive. Like a brick wall.

Out in the yard.
A couple of scary dudes eye me down
One has a tear tattoo under his eye
Remember someone once told me that's code for 'I took a life'.

Scares the shit out of AJ.

He walks around me. Slowly.
I just look at the ground,
don't make eye contact,
Kick some pebbles around.
Pretend I don't notice.

Then—
Big commotion over the east side
Everyone legs it.
A sea of green tracksuits moving in.
What's going on?

AJ *is a bit shaky.*

See some guy on the ground bleeding from the head,
Happens in a flash
He's all messed up
Just lying there
Fuck!

Screws come in screaming
And we're all locked up again
Yard over.

Lie on my bunk
Reckon Coach Peter and the guys are on the footy trip by now

Kicking balls
Logan making dumb jokes
Can't think about that.

Cellmates,
barely a word.
They might be big motherfuckers,
hard-arses,

but they just play cards and talk shit.

Lie on my bunk, thinking about stuff.
Or not.
Just thinking about nothing is good.

Some sort of mince and potato for dinner.
At five p.m.

Then the long, long night locked up starts again.

I'm thinking about how Dani's perfume reminds me of something

Vanilla.
Nailed it
Yep, vanilla ice cream!

Then …

There's just this feeling, and I look up.
The big guy is looking at me.
Standing over me.
Other one's watching on.

Try to look cool.
But my left eye twitches
Big guy puts his hand on my shoulder.
It stays there.
Slides down my upper arm.
Squeezes it so the blood stops.

Bald guy has a wire; he's coming over …

Fuck they're going to fucking slit my throat.
I'm scrambling, but the big guy picks me up with one hand, carries me to the other side of the cell. Where the guards can't see.

'Hey guys

What the fuck?'

Baldy:
'You know what you are?'

I just stare at him.
What the fuck does he mean?
He hits me across the face
Stinging,
hard
cold.
Hit like the sort of hit you don't see coming when you're a kid.

It knocks the wind out of me.

'Answer me when I ask you something.'

Shock.
Mouth won't work.

'A baby boy is what you are.'

I'm trying to find a footing, but he twists my leg and I think it's going to snap.

'No, don't'
My fucking leg.
Stop it.
I play football.
You'll fuck up my leg and my kick.
Another punch to the face.

Blood.

Tasting blood in my mouth.
I'm pushed to the ground.

Main guy flips me over,
my face is up hard against the floor.

My pants
I can't register what's happening.

'Guys'

A laugh,
my legs pulled apart.
Too far

'No, no don't. Don't do this. Fucking don't do this.'

The big guy tells me to keep my mouth shut or they'll slit my throat.

The wire is tucked in under my chin.
They mean it.
They're going to fucking kill me.

Pain.
Up my arse;
like I've never felt.
All the way to my lungs.
I'm struggling;
wire tightens.

Big guy's cock goes all the way through me.
I'm like a rabbit in a trap,
scrambling but not moving anywhere.
Wire at my chin.
I'm screaming but my mouth is jammed against the floor.
Somewhere in my mind,
John the guy at the cop shop:

'Don't let them rip your arsehole.'

But I can't think.
It goes on and on, I'm screaming but I'm not.
Baldy holds my face down hard.
Big guy explodes inside me.
Grunts.
Rolls off.

It's over.
I've been raped.

It's happened.

Mind's racing
What just happened?

I'm trying to pull my legs together, but they're still holding them.

All I can think about is crawling away.
Getting to my bunk.

Then.
No. NO.
It's happening again.
Mind splits into two.
Big guy is now on my leg, my leg is cramping.
A hand slams on my mouth.
Can't breathe.
Another—
I want them to just slit my throat.

Do it. Cut my throat.

Just kill me.
But the pain.
It goes on.
Like it will never stop.

Hand slips from my mouth.

'Kill me'
But they don't.

They flip me over.
Big guy pulls out his cock
again.

In my face.
Clench my teeth.
No way.

No fucking way.

Number two has his wire up close to my chin.
Cuts my neck a little.

I want to die.
My face is slapped from both sides.
Then …

When he rams himself inside my mouth I can't breathe.
For real.

I remember John,
'Relax your muscles' he said
What kind of cunt tells you to relax with a dirty great dick shoved down your throat.

Gagging.
Choking.

'Please god let me die.'

'Or don't let me die.'

I'm not even sure which.

He pulls out of my mouth.

Pulls me up by the hair.
I'm choking on cum.
He's speaking in my ear.

'You're a little cocksucker, aren't you?'

Gag, and spit.

'You wanna go again? Is that it?'

Crawl away.

He keeps pulling me by the hair right back to that spot.

I feel something leaking out of my bum.

Edges of my mouth are ripped and bleeding.

They tell me to say 'I'm your little cocksucker'
And I'll do anything to get away.
It's just I can't speak.

I can't open my mouth.

I can't think straight.

All I can think of is getting to my bunk and under the blanket.

Say it.

'I'm your little cocksucker.'

Then they throw me back on the bunk.

I know I'm sobbing because I can hear myself.

Hear them laughing.
'Get used to it, bitch.'

Baldy comes to the bunk.
I freeze.
No.
He leans in.
I close my eyes and bury my head.

In my ear, I can feel his spit.
'You snitch to any cunt,
You're gonna wind up hanging from your fucking bunk
you hear me?'

I nod.

'Answer me when I speak to you.

You hear me, baby boy?'

'Yes yes.'

I lie very still.

I am not here.

I don't exist.

I get a kick in the face in the morning.

'Rise and shine, baby boy.'

SCENE 20

Ding dong.

COP: Well, is that Mr Seth Rawlins?

SETH: Why?

COP: You're just the young man I wanted to see.

SETH: Why? Mum?

MRS R *rushes down. Sees the* COP. *Moves* SETH *away, anxious.*

MRS R: Seth upstairs now.
Call Dad.

SETH *backs away but doesn't move.*

MRS R: Can I help you?

COP: Mrs Rawlins.

MRS R: Yes, um, now is not a good time, Constable.

COP: It won't take long. Can I come in?
Just need a few words with the young fella here.

MRS R *doesn't open door.*

MRS R: Look I've helped you out already,
My son is not available at the moment.

Seth, I said go upstairs.

SETH *doesn't move.*

COP: I thought you'd appreciate me coming to you rather than asking you to the station!

MRS R: Do we need legal representation?

COP: Not unless you're thinking of being arrested.

He laughs.

MRS R *and* SETH *freeze.*

COP *holds up a paper bag.*

Throws it to SETH *who is surprised that he caught it.*

Just returning the 'famous' Socceroo jersey.
Apparently it's vintage, signed and worth quite a bit according to our evidence guy.

SETH *takes it out of the bag.* MRS R *is delighted, relieved.*

MRS R: Oh the jersey.
You got it back!
Seth—a thank-you?

He looks at it, there is a tear in it.

SETH: There's a rip in it! That's really shit, now it's not worth as much.

MRS R: Seth. The policeman has been good enough to return it, just be grateful you got it back.

SETH: But see this rip, and this mark
And the tag is gone!
This makes the whole top worthless now.

COP: Thought it had sentimental value, mate—

MRS R: Yes it most definitely does—

SETH: It's worthless like this.

COP *can't figure out* SETH. *Look at* MRS R.

COP: We closed the case. Closed!
We went to court;
the guy you ID'd pleaded guilty.
Took himself off to prison!

MRS R: Prison, the young one?

COP: He's off the streets now.
No more break-ins for him.

MRS R: But you said you just needed him to get the other two.
Get the name of the one with the knife.

MRS R: When I picked him out
you said you were just going to use him to get the others.

COP *shrugs.*

So he's in prison for how long?

COP: Think about two to three years if he behaves himself!

MRS R: Two or three years. He was a kid. Just like Seth
You said he might get community service or a suspended sentence?

COP: Not up to me, the courts decide.

MRS R: I told you he said sorry. He looked at me, he looked terrified and he said 'I'm sorry'.

COP: Well he pleaded guilty!
You do the crime, you do the time!

MRS R: Which prison?

COP *looks at* SETH *standing behind his mum.*

COP: Your mum here is a bit soft, hey, mate?

MRS R: Can I visit him?

COP *looks weirded out.*

COP: If you want to find him, talk to Prison Services, not me.

MRS R: I will be.
I will talk to them.
Two to three years, he was just a kid.

Beat. MRS R *takes this all in. Sits down or leans against something.*

COP *looks past* MRS R *again—inside the house and to* SETH.

COP: Insurance came through alright then?

SETH: Yeah.
We got a brand-new TV.

COP: Terrific. What sort?

SETH: A Samsung smart TV—way better than the one we lost!

COP: There you go then.
All's well that ends well.

SCENE 21

AJ *is bent over crying in pain.*

Is it happening again?

Then we realise a NURSE *is examining him.*

NURSE: You have an anal fissure.
Do you know what that is?

AJ *shakes his head.*

AJ: [*inner voice*] Medical
She's writing stuff down.

NURSE: The damage is significant.
You'll need antibiotics,
And I'll give you a laxative so you don't have pain defecating.
Have you had a bowel movement since the 'injury'?

AJ: [*inner voice*] Say nothing.
Look around.
Checking out what I could steal from medical—scissors?
I'm dreaming of a knife.

NURSE: The bleeding has stalled
But you don't want a repeat performance.
You could end up with permanent damage.

AJ: —

NURSE: If you want to make a report, I'll attach the medical notes to it.
Do you want to?
Unless you do, you're stuck in that cell with them.

AJ: —

[*Inner voice*] Think of all the boys on the football trip.
Fuck them.

Laughing on the fucking bus.
Throwing balls around.

NURSE: Andre! I need you to answer me.

AJ: Yes.
No. nothing happened.

NURSE: Something most certainly happened.

AJ: I just woke up like this.

NURSE: Right.
So you're not disclosing the incident?
You're going to let them do this to you again?

AJ: [*inner voice*] Say nothing.
Fucking bitch.
You know nothing.

NURSE: How many times before you're prepared to formally report them?

NURSE *washes* AJ*'s face, puts a sticky thing on the side of his mouth.*

Not gentle but just the touch of it.

AJ *wants to cry.*

Even though it stings.

AJ: [*inner voice*] Think about Dani
Her soft hands.

AJ *starts to cry.*

NURSE: I can get the CSOs to send you to protective custody.

AJ *shakes his head.*

It if happens again you'll be begging to go.

AJ: Nup. I'm good.

[*Inner voice*] But she's right.

The next day
I'm begging.

[*To* NURSE] Get me out of there. Please. Or I'll, I'll kill myself.

NURSE: You have something to report?

AJ: No. Please, don't send me back.

NURSE: Report?

AJ: Help me. Anything …

NURSE *sighs.*

NURSE: Well I can refer you to short-term protective custody.

AJ: Let me think.

NURSE: They'll only take you for a few days.

She hesitates.

But 'things' happen in there too, Andre.
And, you should also know—when you return to your cell
They'll know you talked and …

AJ: [*inner voice*] She doesn't have to say it.

[*To* NURSE] I just want to go home.
I have one year and ten-and-a-half months left before I can be paroled.

NURSE *shrugs.*

NURSE: If you make a complaint, we can *try* and take it further.
Takes a while.
And no guarantees.

AJ: [*inner voice*] Look around for a knife, a beautiful sharp knife I can grab.
A scalpel
Please
But there's nothing.

NURSE: Well?

AJ *shakes his head.*

You'll just feel a small prick of the needle. I'm just taking blood.

Checking for HIV.

> AJ *hangs his head.*
>
> *Can barely feel anything, can't face anyone.*

SCENE 22

SILL *puts his arm on* AJ*'s arm.*

SILL: You know who I am?

AJ: My cellmate.

SILL: Name's Sill
I'm bossman around here.

AJ: I know.

SILL: Come with me

AJ: No, please.

> SILL *starts to pull his arm.*

No. Where are you taking me?

SILL: Come with me or the boys over there'll drag you over.
You and me are going to chat.

AJ: No. No. No.
Will you just kill me, please. Please.

SILL: We can make a deal.

AJ: What?

SILL: You want protection? Access to contra? I get favours.

AJ: What kind of favours?

SILL: No more blood.
Because you would be my property.
And I protect what is mine.

AJ: What about Baldy
The other guy in our cell?

SILL: Once word's out you're my property—anyone else tries it, I kill 'em.

AJ: How … often … ?

SILL: As often as I want.

AJ: But I'm not, I'm not …

SILL: The offer is now or never.

AJ: Now or never.

SILL: Yes now, or it's over to the others.

AJ: Now or never.

SILL: Yes or no?

AJ *answers with a look, he is broken, destroyed yet weirdly grateful—he nods his answer.*

SCENE 23

AJ: Who are you?

MRS R: Hello, Andre?

AJ: Are you trying to make me believe in God.

MRS R: No.

AJ: Because if you try I'm walking right out of here.

MRS R: Okay.

Beat.

You've lost your shoelaces I see.

AJ: So we don't hang ourselves.

MRS R: Oh, that's awful.

AJ: [*darkly*] Yeah, I'd give anything to be able to hang myself.

—

Who are you?

MRS R: My name's Joanne.

AJ: —

MRS R: I just wanted to make sure you were doing okay in here?

AJ: Are you a social worker?

MRS R: No. But are you doing okay? Are things … comfortable in here?

AJ: In here? Comfortable?
Who the fuck are you?

MRS R: I wanted to visit you.
I needed you to know that I forgive you.

AJ: You said no religion!

MRS R: No. I mean for breaking into our house and taking everything.

AJ: You're the woman on the stairs.

MRS R: We were very shaken by it.
Very upset.
And I hurt my shoulder.
But I remember you said 'sorry' on the night.

AJ: I said what?

MRS R: You said 'I'm sorry'.
I wanted you to know that I told the police you said that;
I said I didn't think you were the ringleader.
I knew that by looking at you.

Beat.

And I just—
I also feel a bit …

AJ: —

MRS R: I have a son your age.
He's just turned eighteen actually.

AJ: [*hidden sarcasm*] Happy birthday to him!

MRS R: Thank you.
You look well.
I just wanted to know that you were making the most of it in here?

AJ *stares back in disbelief. It's unnerving for* MRS R.

I mean like getting some qualifications and some therapy, some help?

AJ: Sure am.

MRS R: That's great.

AJ: Yeah.
I'm talking to a psychologist on Mondays
Doing dance classes every Tuesday

MRS R: Dance!
That's wonderful.

AJ: And the rest of the week I spend with my mates here
Met some great guys.

MRS R: Really?

AJ: Also planning for the future, doing some study.

MRS R: Andre, I am so thrilled to—

AJ: Yeah. It's going great.
I'm studying to be a brain surgeon.
Prison officers let me practise on their heads every Friday.

MRS R: —

AJ: It's great in here
I never ever want to leave.

Was it you who ID'd me?
Put me in here?

MRS R: Please, Andre. I didn't mean for you to go to prison.
They said it was the way to get the guy with the knife, but …
I just wanted to make sure nothing bad has happened to you in here.
That's all.

AJ *flinches, he stares in her face.*

Their eyes meet.

MRS R *is not getting the answer she wanted.*

Something has happened to him.

You have to believe me.
I'm sorry, I wish I hadn't …
I thought—
I don't know what I thought.

She reaches out to him. He pulls away.

What days does your mum come in to visit?

This does AJ *in.*

He has hot hot tears behind his eyes.

AJ: Would you put your own son in here?
That kid who just turned eighteen?
WOULD YOU?
Because I'm not here doing dance fucking classes
I'm here losing my mind
Looking over my shoulder every second of every day
Eating shit
Getting—

Dealing with—

You got no idea !

Or maybe you do.
And you let it happen anyway?
As long as it's not your precious kid.

MRS R: It's not up to me, Andre.
And if you hadn't broken into my home …

AJ: Yeah I guess your fucking perfect son
never makes mistakes.

MRS R: Look.
If there's anything I could do …

AJ: Yeah well I reckon there is.

MRS R *leans in.*

You know what you can do?
You can go fuck yourself, lady.

[*Calling out*] Guard.

AJ *leaves.*

MRS R *sits there, watching him walk away.*

SCENE 24

AJ: [*inner voice*] Make the fucking most of it!
MAKE THE MOST OF IT!

Five months and six days to go.

No-one fucking visits me
Bloody Mum
Such a flake

Dani why won't you come and see me?

I lift another barbell
Up to a hundred KGs now
Check out my bod.
Starting to look like a dude not to mess with.

Turns out last year I had a sign on my fucking forehead that said 'Fuck me'.

Or something.

Not now.
Got it figured out now
Different head on my shoulders.

Thinking maybe I could still play a bit when I get out?
With this strong bod
Could still kick goals.

A postcard comes in for my birthday

From Mum. My birthday was last week
But she craps on about how much she loves me.
Reckons I could come live with her when I'm out.
Then says the deal is I'd have to do the dishes every night.

Actually sounds like a fucken luxury to be honest.

Footsteps in the gym.
It's Sill.
Body goes cold, just automatically.

I don't think about it.
I hate it but just be this robot.
Do it
Don't think about it.
He's quick.

I have to say shit.
Fucked-up shit.

I'm not a fucking gay dude.

I'm just something that he owns I guess.
Sill's boy.
And no-one fucks with his property.
No-one.
That's my insurance right there.

Keeps me safe.

SCENE 25

DANI: You look different.
Good different.

COACH: You're looking great, mate.
You could play goalie as well as striker now!

AJ: Yeah?
Thanks for coming in, you two.

COACH: No problem.
It's good to see you, AJ.

AJ: Yeah. Yeah.
What's new?

COACH: Not much.

DANI: Logan got a pro deal!

AJ: Logan?

COACH *shoots* DANI *a look.*

Scouts pick him up then?

COACH: Nothing's certain, mate.

DANI: Oh, yeah.
Nothing's certain.

AJ: Good. Cos I can whip his arse.

COACH: Course you can.

COACH *smiles at him with sympathy.*

AJ *doesn't like this.*

DANI: I need you to get out soon.

DANI *leans in.*

We're still moving in right?
Told my mum we were going to Queensland
She thought I was preggas!

She laughs.

AJ: Reckon you will be soon as I'm out.

DANI *beams.*

[*Inner voice*] I smell her vanilla perfume.
It's amazing.
Makes me think about ice cream.
Coach used to hand them out when we won a game.

I was such a fucking baby.
I feel that hot feeling behind my eyes.
No way.

Can't go back there,
those days are gone.

DANI: Mum asked if you're gonna put a ring on it?

AJ: Dunno. If you want.

[*Inner voice*] I glance at Coach.
Why's he giving me a weird look?

Can other fags see if someone has been fucked up the arse?

Probably.
[*To* DANI] You look hot, Dani.
When I get out of here
I'm going to fuck you for a week.

[*Inner voice*] Dani rolls her eyes,
but she likes it.

DANI: You been working out?

AJ: Sure have.
Up to a hundred KGs now

Bet you can't lift that, Coach?
Hey?
Not even in your so-called pro days I reckon.

COACH: What do you mean
'so-called'?

AJ: The men in here, now they can lift!

Check these babies out, Dan.

He shows her his guns.

Really shows them off.

AJ *looks at* COACH.

Not you.
You don't get to look.

COACH *leans back.*

Not happy.

DANI *looks nervous.*

COACH: Are things okay for you in here, AJ?

AJ: [*inner voice*] He knows.
Fuck.

I never used to care that he was fucking gay,
didn't mean nothing!
But—
Now.

Oh fuck.
He can tell.
I think he can see shit.
He knows what's going on.

COACH: There's these new football scholarships, might be a long shot but …
you interested?

AJ: Nah.
No point,
too old now.

DANI: You said you were going pro.

COACH: I spoke to the club, put in a word for you.

AJ: Don't go fucking talking about me to no-one.

COACH: Okay then.

DANI: He was doing it for you, AJ.

AJ: [*inner voice*] Coach fucking knows.

Knows something.

[*To* COACH] Stop looking at me like that, arsehole.

But COACH *keeps looking at* AJ, *he won't be told what to do.*

I said stop staring at me
There's nothing for you here

You got it?

COACH: You watch yourself, AJ.

AJ: [*inner voice*] Next thing I'm saying things to Coach that I've never even thought about him.
Not once in my life did I give a rat's that he was gay.

[*To* COACH] So what are you looking at, poofta?
Never really believed in me, didya?
You only ever wanted some cock, I know how fags like you think.
But I'm a fucking MAN, you hear me.
You can get Logan to suck your cock.
I don't want no fucking gay coach staring at me.

DANI: AJ! What are you doing?

AJ: Faggot. You looking at me like that.
Like you want to do me.

COACH: Shut the fuck up or I'm leaving.

AJ: I don't do fags, you hear me.
I don't fucking talk to fags like you.
You all want one thing.

AJ *feels cornered.*

No-one holding him down, but he feels like there is.

[*Inner voice*] I go further, and further.
Every name I ever heard.
His face is getting really dark.
He tells me to go fuck myself.

I want to hug Coach Peter, like I used to when I was a kid and I kicked a goal
But I never will again,
I know this now.
Scream words at him.

[*To* COACH] Faggots shouldn't be coaching boys' and mens' football.

[*Inner voice*] Other cons around me are looking, so are their visitors.

DANI: You're an arsehole.

AJ: [*Inner voice*] When I tell him to get the fuck out of here,
I know he is already gone.

COACH *and* DANI *fade into the background.*

COACH *stands up.*

Gives AJ *a look—*

AJ *knows that look.*

DANI *scuttles off behind him.*

Throws AJ *a dirty glance.*

AJ *doesn't care.*

It feels good to hurt someone.
To do it and feel it.

For once.

SCENE 26

AJ: [*inner voice*] No-one to meet me at the gate
Jump on the bus.

Thought I would be so happy to be out.

But—
Nothing at all.

Social gave me a junior job as a security guard.
Guy who runs it gets a cut of my 'post-incarceration' salary.
Social worker reckons because my conviction had violence in it, I can't work in sporting clubs.

Look out the window.
Watch people walk on the streets.
Like it's normal to be free.

Bus moves through toward the city, ends up at the old interchange.
A new café nearby.

I've got twenty bucks and my life in a plastic bag.

Seeing Dani on the weekend.

She's still mad about me being 'disrespectful' when she visited.
But she reckons it's cool to think about me not having had sex for two years.

Beat.

Coach Peter got a job with Melbourne Victory, moved south.
No biggie.
—
New guy at the football club said I can come by and kick some balls.
Maybe I could work my way up to play in a team there …
—
The security job starts on Thursday night.

A shift every night for the entire week.
Get some money.

See a girl on the street.
Ask her for a smoke.
She says 'buy your own'.

Cunt.

SCENE 27

MRS R *helps* SETH *put on a t-shirt.*

It's pink with surfers on it.

MRS R: I thought you could wear it tonight.
I saw it and thought it was perfect.

SETH: But I like the button-ups.
This is a surfer's t-shirt.

MRS R: It's just a bit more casual, Seth.
More appropriate for tonight.
Big celebration with your schoolfriends.
End of exams!
And if your trial marks are anything to go by

You've done brilliantly, darling.

SETH: I don't surf.

MRS R: The young lady from maths class, will she be there tonight?

SETH: Yes.

MRS R: Is Bash taking a date?

SETH: Probably.

MRS R: It's a double date then!

SETH: Maybe. It's gonna be expensive.

MRS R: Do you need some extra money?

SETH: Should I offer to pay for her?

MRS R: Very chivalrous, Seth.
Here, let me give you enough to go somewhere nice.

Have you thought about asking her to the school formal?

SETH: I don't go to those things.

MRS R: But it's the last one. You must go, darling.
And this time you have someone to ask.

SETH: I can't afford the tickets.

MRS R: Dad and I'll pay.
I'll put the money into your account right away.
But you have to let me take photos on the night.

SETH: Well …

MRS R: Please.

SETH: Will you give me my Switch back?
Now?

MRS R: Will you ask your friend to go with you to the formal?

Beat.

SETH: Deal.

MRS R *secretly hands* SETH *the Switch as he leaves.*

SETH *is so happy to see it, puts it in his bag.*

As … MR R *comes in with two glasses of wine.*

MRS R: Tom
Seth's leaving for a big night out.

MR R: A toast.

MRS R: Definitely.

MR R: Here's to Seth.
Great maths marks in the trials
University choices should be wide.

MRS R: He's taking a young lady with him tonight, Tom.

MR R: Well that's terrific.

MRS R: Are you going to give us her name?

MR R: Enough, Jo.
Leave the boy alone
He's a man now.
Enjoy it, Seth.
Wink wink, son.

SETH *drinks then leaves.*

SETH: See ya.

The parents call out 'bye' and then look at each other, proudly.

MR R *shrugs.*

Pours some wine.

MR R: Here's to us, darling.
We got there in the end.
All that drugs palaver just a blip in the past
he's on the right track now.
Graduating!

MRS R: Yeah.

She is looking very melancholic.

MR R: What?

Jo, stop thinking about that boy in jail.

MRS R: I can't.

MR R: You never should have gone in there.

MRS R: He looked so haunted, Tom,
And I was the one who picked him out of the line-up.

MR R: Jo, it's not your fault!

MRS R: Okay so, whose is it?

MR R: Hey. This is Seth's night, our night.
Come on.

A moment. Is she going to say more?

No.

Clink glasses.

She smiles.

SCENE 28

Outside the club.

There is a clap or a sound effect to mark when one character finishes speaking and the other must quicky jumped in. This is especially significant if the same actor plays both AJ *and* SETH.

AJ: I need IDs before you can go in.
Thanks.

And you?

No ID, no entry.

Sorry, mate.

[*Inner voice*] One week in
Feeling good.

Got paid yesterday.
Like literally money in my account.

Tomorrow night Dani's place.
Big night I reckon.
She still wants to talk about Queensland

Mum's birthday's on Sunday
Bought her a present today

She pats me on the back,
'You're doing good, AJ.'
Which was—

Yeah.

Pretty girl smiles at me.
In her red dress, long hair—
Flicks her hair and goes in.

I'm the king of the castle,
I decide who can come in or not.

Barman tells me it's full.

So now it's a one-out-one-in thing.

SETH: [*inner voice*] Walk two streets up and
Bash's on the corner waiting for me.
Cool.
We got business tonight.

Mum was right.
No button-up shirt
Bash's wearing jeans and a T-shirt.

Sold my signed football jersey on Marketplace.
Hardly got anything for it.
Would have got almost half my airfare to Japan if the guy that stole it hadn't ripped the neckline.
Arsehole.

Once Bash and I cash up tonight,
I'm all done.

That's the money for my airfare, plus extra to set up a flat in Japan.
Thank god I'm leaving the country before the formal comes around so Mum'll never know that I made up the girl from maths class.

Bash and me walk to the club
Stand in the line
Waiting.

AJ: [*inner voice*] People in the line groan,
some leave.
The ones who really want to get in,
asking me questions.

'Why?'

'How long?'

Tell me it doesn't look packed.
'New rules,' I say.
One guy
Gives me a filthy look.
Like I'm management.

Feel a rise
Push it down.
A group of three comes out,
I'm telling them if they leave that's it.

Girl with cute tush
wiggles her butt.
Her long black hair swishes.
Smiles at me.
I let her and her two girlfriends in.

SETH: Hey, he let those three in before us?!
[*Inner voice*] Feel Bash getting antsy too.

He's texting the Big Timer inside
Guy's gonna sell us a bucketload of drugs so we can make a killing

Bash says the guy's name is Xcel
like the spreadsheet.
Got a tattoo on his head. Weird.

Bash tells me to 'say nothing' when we do the deal.
Says 'act cool bro' in front of the Big Timer.

Bash'll do all the talking, like usual, and I'll do all the adding up.
Then we'll both deliver the goods.
Like we did with the Ritalin that time.
Don't wanna stand out here
What if the cops come?

This is real money now.
Proper deal.
I'll be rolling in it when I get to Tokyo.

I want to get my Switch out but I know people will think that's weird at a club at night.
Bash asks the security guy 'How much longer?'

AJ: 'Fuck off mate, you're in when you're in.'

[*Inner voice*] Guy hassles me to get in

His mate's wearing a pink T-shirt
something about a surf club.
Weird surf dude's looking at me. I don't like it.
'Hey, mate, what are you looking at?
You two stay back.
I got my eye on you.
Wait your turn, you hear me!'
Weird guy stares at me.
His mate throws me a dirty one.

SETH: [*inner voice*] Want Bash to know I can hold my own.
I ask the security guy,
'What's the fucking problem?
We were here first. We wanna get in.'
Bash'll have my back, I know that.

'You let those chicks in ahead of us, mate.
That's not fair, we were here first?'

Security guy turns his back to me
We need to be inside making money.

Not out here where people might see us.
Sweating.

I wanna get inside.
I tap his shoulder.

AJ: [*inner voice*] Fucken hell.
Hand on my shoulder.

Pulls me towards him.
Fired up.

Wants something.

SETH: [*inner voice*] 'You let those chicks in ahead of us, mate.
That's not fair, we were here first?'
He still doesn't hear me.
The guy turns back around

AJ: [*inner voice*] Fuck, he's trying to come on to me.
Eyes blur,
Feel my gut rising.

He's not letting go
He holds my upper arm.
Tight.
'Let go'
Breathe
'Fuck off, poofta.'

SETH: [*inner voice*] He's yelling at me,
Keep hold of his arm
'We need to go in, we have business in there'

AJ: [*inner voice*] I'm sweating.
the hand is still there
It's tighter

Moves down my arm.
Heart thumping

SETH: [*inner voice*] I move my face to his ear.

'Me and my mate here.

We need to be inside.
I'm not good at waiting'

See Bash watching.
I man up a bit.

'Hey, you. Do you fucking understand me?
Let us in!

AJ: [*inner voice*] Gotta get him away.
Feel like I'm choking.
No.
No.
Then my other arm
Knocks this guy away.

SETH: [*inner voice*] What's …
I don't understand.
I'm moving, flying.
Everything in slow motion.
I can see the lights on the club

AJ: [*inner voice*] Weird guy goes down hard.
What?
His head hits the ground.

SETH: [*inner voice*] Don't want to rip my new jeans.
I need to take these with me to Japan.

AJ: [*inner voice*] I want to run,
But—
Screams
A girl's scream.

SETH: [*inner voice*] Pain, my head.
What's happening?

AJ: [*inner voice*] Kid's down
Not moving much.

SETH: [*inner voice*] Where's my Switch?

AJ: [*inner voice*] Blood.

Screams.
People come out of the club

SETH: [*inner voice*] I wish I'd worn my button-up shirt

AJ: [*inner voice*] Some guy holds on to me
Then another, and another.

I kick like a crazy motherfucker.
Sirens.

SETH: [*inner voice*] What's happening?

AJ: [*inner voice*] Red lights.

SETH: [*inner voice*] Taste blood.

AJ: 'Get the fuck off me'

[*Inner voice*] I'm fighting

Get the fuck off of me

Fucking assholes

Get off me
cocksuckers.

I see the kid's eyes
They're closed

SETH: [*inner voice*] Everything is so slow.

Can't see.
Black.

AJ: [*inner voice*] But his mouth is moving.

Sorry, kid.

Blood.

Sirens.

Blue lights.

People filming

Me

Filming me
Wake up, kid,
wake up.
Fuck. Fuck

Please wake up.

THE END

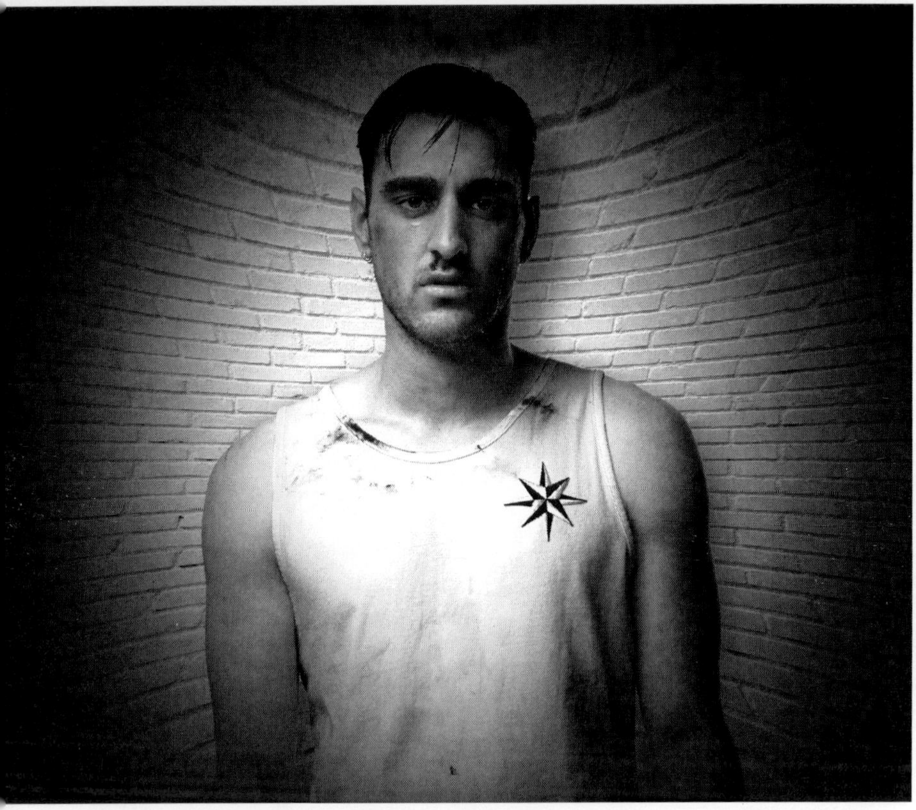

GRIFFIN THEATRE COMPANY PRESENTS

JAILBABY

BY SUZIE MILLER

7 JULY – 12 AUGUST 2023 | SBW STABLES THEATRE

GRIFFIN
THEATRE
COMPANY

Government partners

We would not be where we are today without the vision and generosity of the Seaborn, Broughton & Walford (S,B&W) Foundation, to whom we owe the great privilege of being able to perform in the much-loved SBW Stables Theatre.

CAST & CREATIVES

Director **Andrea James**

Dramaturg **Declan Greene**

Set & Costume Designer **Isabel Hudson**

Lighting Designer **Verity Hampson**

Composer & Sound Designer **Phil Downing**

Stage Manager **Madelaine Osborn**

Intimacy and Consent Consultant
Bayley Turner

With
Lucia Mastrantone
Anthony Taufa
Anthony Yangoyan

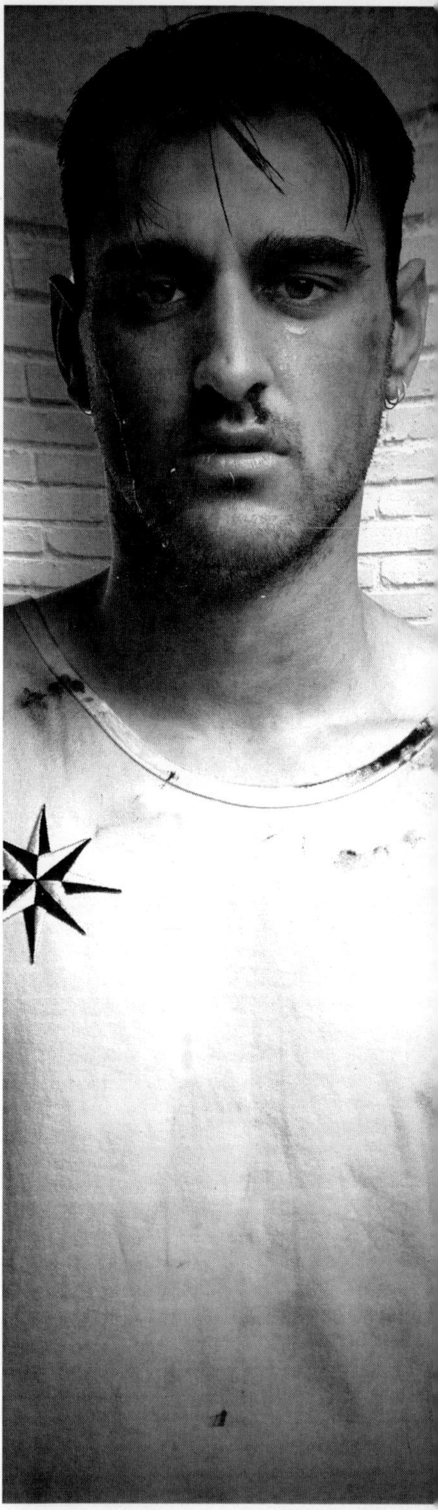

Jailbaby is supported by Griffin's Production Partner program.

This production of *Jailbaby* was supported through a residency at Theatre and Performance Studies, the University of Sydney.

Jailbaby was developed and produced with the assistance of the Australian Writers' Guild David Williamson Prize.

PLAYWRIGHT'S NOTE

The law applies to all regardless of background (but it doesn't).

The state is supposed to step in early where there is inequality or abuse (but it doesn't).

While we all turn a blind eye to human rights abuses in prison systems, there is the awful irony that we all KNOW what happens—and indeed those passing sentences have been known to threaten those before the criminal justice system over what awaits them in prison.

Rape and torture are not part of a prison sentence—but they are what can be reasonably expected, and it goes predominantly without prosecution. We as a community never take umbrage that this is what occurs when our 'squeaky clean' justice system doles out prison time so that the 'rest of us' can live in peace.

Given that the system began as a means of protecting a man's (sic) property (which included that man's wife and children from rape or damage), the law has then evolved such that property theft/damage rather than anything else is the highest form of transgression (other than murder) and therefore receives the highest sentences.

When those who have no property or income infringe upon those who do, then prison it is. When they are in prison, they are paradoxically traded as property, reduced to raw meat, and bartered amongst other prisoners.

As a society, are our ideas around property wrong?

When those destroyed young men leave prison it is not without the scars and anger that lead to violent crimes (that they had previously not had any inclination towards). It is not without rampant homophobia against innocent individuals in the community who played no part in the heterosexual rape of jailbabies in prison. The self-hatred and their experiences of prison life are sources of shame and undermine their sense of self with such ferocity that they must now prove they are 'a man' (i.e. a 'heterosexual') to themselves and the world in the one way they know—by perpetuating more violence against the vulnerable.

This play was written with the support of the brilliant Griffin Theatre Company, the generous support of the David Williamson Award and dramaturgy by **Declan Greene**, with further input from **Andrea James** and **Caleb Lewis**. I hail and thank Griffin Theatre Company once again for its commitment to new Australian works. This first ever season of *Jailbaby* is directed by Andrea James, a Yorta Yorta/Gunaikurnai woman who it has been an honour to work alongside on Gadigal land. Andrea's talent, theatrical language and emotional insights around this work have been invaluable. A director who digs deep, perfectly blending her brilliant mind and heart in her artform, Andrea runs a rehearsal room with respect and humanity at all times.

I also thank the entire creative team and the brilliant cast on this premiere production: **Lucia Mastrantone**, **Anthony Taufa** and **Anthony Yangoyan**. I cannot express the appreciation for the wonderful people who have supported me to write this play: my family: Robert, Gabriel and Sasha; my close and loving friends; my agents: **Zilla Turner** at HLA Management, **Julia Kreitman** and **Tanya Tillett** at The Agency London; **Claire Grady** and **Katie Pollock** at Currency Press; **Jane Sanders** at the Shopfront Youth Legal Centre; and all the Griffin Theatre Company contributors and audiences.

Suzie Miller
Playwright

DIRECTOR'S NOTE

Working with **Suzie Miller** on *Jailbaby* has been like being in the slipstream of a jet airplane. Fresh from the London and Broadway successes of *Prima Facie,* we finally pinned Suzie down to prepare *Jailbaby* for the stage. With her background in human rights law and youth justice, Suzie brings her multiplicitous sensibility and legal expertise to the task.

Ground down by over a decade defending young people in a flawed and inhumane justice system, Suzie shines a light into the darkest corners of incarceration and rigid class systems that entrap us all.

Young vulnerable men—many of whom graduate from juvenile detention to adult prisons—are known as 'jailbabies'; and are subjected to violence and sexual abuse while incarcerated at an alarming rate. A study by **David Heilpern** in 1998 found that up to a quarter of prisoners experience sexual violence and rape in Australian jails with an overrepresentation of people from marginalized communities. With politicians all too eager to lock young offenders up and throw away the key, prison authorities and Australian society turn a blind eye to the 'extra punishment' that regularly occurs in our jails—often in the name of defending the property of the middle classes.

The high and impenetrable walls of adult prisons in Australia belie a world thick with fear and tension; where language, systems and codes of behavior are like nothing experienced on the 'outside'. Stripped of privileges and privacy there is a constant atmosphere of high alert and a stratification of prison society where the abuse of power and force is the most valued and terrifying commodity.

While our jailbaby transforms from an innocent bystander to hardened criminal, Suzie deftly holds a mirror up to another young man—the youngest member of the well-to-do family whose house is robbed. Equally troubled and criminally culpable, the unequal consequences for this young man are plain to see. In a colonial country with a foreign and imposed justice system, you can literally get away with murder if you're on the right side of society's ledger.

And while both of our 'babies' may seem like they are worlds apart, are we all just as trapped by class and commercialism as those who are sent to prison? Is it okay for us to continue to turn a blind eye to sexual violence and human rights abuses in our prisons in the name of keeping society safe and our property protected?

When our worlds collide, we may find that we're not really that different from each other.

Andrea James
Director

BIOGRAPHIES

SUZIE MILLER
PLAYWRIGHT

Suzie Miller is a contemporary international playwright and screenwriter drawn to complex personal stories often exploring injustice. Her plays have been produced in 40 productions around the world and won multiple prestigious awards. She has been commissioned by, or been in residence, at theatres including London's National Theatre, the National Theatre of Scotland, Griffin Theatre Company, Theatre Gargantua Canada and La Boite Theatre. In 2019, her drama *Prima Facie* premiered at Griffin Theatre Company. The play won the 2020 AWGIE Award for Drama, the 2020 David Williamson Award for Outstanding Theatre Writing and the prestigious Major AWGIE across all categories of theatre, film and television. *Prima Facie* enjoyed extraordinary acclaim in 2022, marking Suzie's West End debut produced by Empire Street Productions and starring Jodie Comer before transferring to Broadway in 2023. In 2023, the production had three Tony nominations and won the Tony Award for Best Actress (Jodie Comer); it had four Olivier nominations and won the Olivier Award for Best New Play (Suzie Miller) and Best Actress (Jodie Comer), and won the What'sOnStage Award London for Best New Play. *Prima Facie* has been translated into 20 languages. Other theatre credits include: for Sydney Theatre Company: *RBG: Of Many, One*, for Griffin: *Caress/Ache*; for Griffin Independent: *Sunset Strip*; for Black Swan State Theatre Company: *DUST*; for La Boite Theatre: *The Mathematics of Longing*, *Medea*; for Performing Lines WA: *Overexposed*; for Perth International Arts Festival: *Driving Into Walls*, *OneFiveZeroSeven*; for Queensland Opera: *Snow White*; for Ransom Theatre Northern Ireland & Seymour Centre/Riverside Theatres: *Transparency*. Other international credits include: for Assembly Rooms for Theatre 503 (UK): *SOLD*; for the Cherry Tree Theatre (USA): *Reasonable Doubt*; for the National Theatre of Scotland: *Velvet Evening Séance*; and for Theatre Gargantua (Canada): *The Sacrifice Zone*. Among other awards, Suzie has been awarded the Kit Denton Award for Writing with Courage in 2009, the 2018 Griffin Award, the NY Fringe Festival Overall Excellence Award for Outstanding Playwriting, the AWGIE for Radio Playwriting, Inscription (and a mentorship with Edward Albee in 2006 and 2009) and more. Most recently, Suzie has written a feature film adaptation of *Prima Facie* for Bunya Productions and Participant Media in the US, with Cynthia Erivo to star in and serve as Executive Producer.

ANDREA JAMES

DIRECTOR

Andrea is a Yorta Yorta/Gunaikurnai theatremaker and graduate of the Victorian College of the Arts. She was Artistic Director of Melbourne Workers Theatre from 2001–2008 where she is best known for her play *Yanagai! Yanagai!* The play premiered at Playbox in 2004, was remounted in 2006 and toured to the UK. Andrea was the Aboriginal Arts Development Officer at Blacktown Arts Centre from 2010–2012 and was the Aboriginal Producer at Carriageworks from 2012–2016 before going freelance. She was recipient of British Council's Accelerate Program for Aboriginal Art Leaders in 2013 and was awarded the Create NSW Aboriginal Arts Fellowship in 2018. Andrea wrote and directed *Winyanboga Yurringa* at Carriageworks and Geelong Performing Arts Centre in 2016, remounted at Belvoir in 2019. Her play *Sunshine Super Girl*, about Wiradjuri tennis star Evonne Goolagong-Cawley, premiered in Griffith in 2020, enjoyed a season at the 2021 Sydney Festival, underwent an extensive national tour in 2022 and was nominated for four Green Room Awards. Her play *Dogged* was written with collaborator Catherine Ryan and premiered at Griffin Theatre Company in May 2021. Andrea is currently Associate Artistic Director at Griffin, directing *Ghosting the Party* by Melissa Bubnic in May 2022. Andrea was recently awarded the Mona Brand Award for Women Stage and Screen Writers—Australia's most prestigious writing prize for women.

ISABEL HUDSON

SET & COSTUME DESIGNER

Isabel is an award-winning set and costume designer. Isabel's design credits for the stage include: for Griffin: *Ghosting the Party*, *Pony*; for Belvoir: *Blessed Union*, *Every Brilliant Thing*, *Winyanboga Yurringa*; for Belvoir 25A: *Jess & Joe Forever*, *Tuesday*; for Hayes Theatre Co: *Razorhurst, The View Upstairs*; for Melbourne Theatre Company: *Torch the Place*; for New Theatricals: *Darkness*; for NIDA: *Mr Burns*; for Pinchgut Opera: *Farnace*; for Sydney Festival/Rising/Darwin Festival: *Maureen: Harbinger of Death*; and for Sydney Theatre Company: *Hubris & Humiliation*. Isabel's set design credits include: for Hayes Theatre Co: *American Psycho*, *Cry-Baby*, *Young Frankenstein*. She was the costume designer and associate set designer for *The Mousetrap* (Crossroads Productions). Isabel has won the Sydney Theatre Award for Best Set Design of an Independent Production two years in a row—for the musicals *American Psycho* and *Cry-Baby* at Hayes Theatre Co, which went on to tour to Sydney Opera House. Isabel also won the APDG Award for Best Set Design for *American Psycho*. Isabel is the Australian Set Associate for *Moulin Rouge! The Musical* Australia, Korea and Japan. She was recently awarded the Kristian Fredrikson Scholarship and the Thelma Louise Award. Isabel holds a Bachelor of Design from NIDA and a Bachelor of Arts (Screen and Sound) from the University of New South Wales.

VERITY HAMPSON

LIGHTING DESIGNER

Verity's lighting designs for theatre include: for Griffin: *A Strategic Plan*, *And No More Shall We Part*, *Angela's Kitchen*, *Beached, Dealing With Clair, Dogged, Ghosting the Party*, *Orange Thrower, Pony*, *The Bleeding Tree*, *The Boys*, *The Bull, The Moon and the Coronet of Stars*, *The Floating World*, *Superheroes*, *This Year's Ashes*, *The Turquoise Elephant*; for Griffin Independent: *The Brothers Size*, *The Cold Child*, *Crestfall*, *Family Stories: Belgrade*, *Live Acts On Stage*, *Music*, *The New Electric Ballroom*, *References to Salvador Dali Make Me Hot*, *Way to Heaven*; for Griffin/Bell Shakespeare: *The Literati*; for Bell Shakespeare: *A Midsummer Night's Dream*, *Julius Caesar*, *Titus Andronicus*; for Belvoir: *An Enemy of the People*, *The Blind Giant is Dancing*, *The Drover's Wife*, *Faith Healer*, *Ivanov*, *Sami in Paradise*, *Winyanboga Yurringa*; for Black Swan/Sydney Theatre Company: *City of Gold*; for CAAP/Sydney Festival: *Double Delicious*; for Dancenorth: *Dungarri Nya Nya*; for Ensemble Theatre: *A Doll's House*, *Baby Doll*, *Fully Committed*, *The One*; for Hayes Theatre Co: *Lizzie*; for Malthouse Theatre: *Wake in Fright*; for Queensland Theatre: *Death of a Salesman*; and for Sydney Theatre Company: *7 Stages of Grieving*, *A Raisin in the Sun*, *Blackie Blackie Brown*, *Fences*, *Grand Horizons*, *Hamlet: Prince of Skidmark*, *Home, I'm Darling*, *Machinal*, *Little Mercy*. Verity is a recipient of the Mike Walsh Fellowship and has won three Sydney Theatre Awards, a Green Room Award and an APDG Award for Best Lighting Design.

PHIL DOWNING

COMPOSER & SOUND DESIGNER

Phil has been performing and recording music for over 20 years, and was first engaged to produce soundtracks for theatre through experimentation with original musical inventions. Phil's credits include: for Griffin: *Ghosting the Party*; for Alice Osbourne/ Performance Space: *Falling*; for Branch Nebula: *Artwork, Crush, High Performance Packing Tape, STOP-GO*; for Erth: *Murder*; for Moogahlin Performing Arts: *Rainbow's End, The Visitors, This Fella My Memory, Winyanboga Yurringa*; for My Darling Patricia: *Posts in the Paddock, The Piper*; for Side Pony Productions: *The Irresistible*; and for Vicky Van Hout: *Long Grass, Plenty Serious Talk Talk*, *Stolen*. Phil continues composing using various music recording/editing tools, creating sounds from found objects or manipulation of surroundings and the natural environment.

MADELAINE OSBORN

STAGE MANAGER

Madelaine is a theatremaker living and working on Gadigal and Wiradjuri land. In 2015, she graduated from Charles Sturt University's B. Communication: Theatre/Media course with Distinction and was the 2015 recipient of the Blair Milan Memorial Scholarship. Madelaine's stage management credits include: for Griffin: *Ghosting the Party*, Batch Festival, *Is There Something Wrong With That Lady?*; for Griffin/Black Birds: *Exhale*; for Australian Theatre for Young People: *Follow Me Home* (Riverside Theatres 2019 Season and 2021 Tour), *INTERSECTION: Arrival*; for Branch Nebula: *Air Time*; for Nell Ranney/Victoria Haralabidou: *GRLZ*; and for Performing Lines: *Sunshine Super Girl* (National Tour). As assistant stage manager, her credits include: for Pinchgut Opera: *Gisutino*, *Medée*, *The Loves of Daphne and Apollo*. Madelaine is passionate about creating new Australian work that is accessible and empowering to minority groups and communities that may not regularly be exposed to theatre and performance art. She is delighted to be returning to the SBW Stables Theatre this year.

BAYLEY TURNER

INTIMACY & CONSENT CONSULTANT

Bayley Turner is a proud queer trans woman, writer, performer, and consent advocate. As the founder and driving force behind *Create Consent*, Bayley's work involves consulting with creative production teams on consent-centred creative practices, policy and protocol documentation and facilitating bespoke workshops locally and internationally with theatre and film projects. Having completed her Masters at Monash University with a thesis discussing consent in the creative industries, she went on to conceptualise and organise Consent Festival, which opened the 2019 Midsumma Festival, and has spoken at various local and international conferences. She recently won a MEAA scholarship to train with Alicia Rodis of IDC Professionals in intimacy, compounding her training with Intimacy on Set with Ita O'Brien. She was also accepted into the 2022 'She Starts Out' entrepreneurship program with global consulting firm Ernst & Young. http://create-consent.com/

LUCIA MASTRANTONE

JO RAWLINS, OLIVIA AND OTHERS

Lucia has a successful career in theatre, physical theatre, film, TV and as a voice artist. Most recently Lucia starred in *La Cage Aux Folles* for Showtunes Productions. Lucia last appeared with Griffin Theatre Company in *Window, Cricket Bat,* as well as *Dead Cat Bounce, Kill Climate Deniers* and *Ladies Day*. Select theatre credits include: for Bell Shakespeare: *The Duchess of Malfi*; for Belvoir: *Looking for Alibrandi*, *Atlantis, The Book of Everything*, *The Cherry Orchard*, *Macbeth, My Vicious Angel*, *Scorched, Twelfth Night*; for Darlinghurst Theatre Company: *The Hypochondriac*; for Hayes Theatre Co:

Young Frankenstein; for Melbourne Theatre Company: *The Venetian Twins*; for the State Theatre Company of South Australia: *A Little Like Drowning*, *The Merchant of Venice*, *Six Characters in Search of an Author*, *Verona*; and for Sydney Theatre Company: *The Harp in the South, Mariage Blanc*, *Romeo & Juliet*, *Talk*. In the realm of physical theatre, Lucia's credits include: for Legs on the Wall: *Under the Influence* (Hammersmith, Edinburgh and Europe Tour); for Shaun Parker & Company: *Blue Love* (European/National Tour); and for Urban Theatre Projects: *The Longest Night*. Lucia worked as the Associate Director/Movement Director for *The Baulkham Hills African Ladies Troupe* at Belvoir/Sydney Opera House. On television, Lucia's appearances include: for ABC: *The Letdown*, *Rake*, *Significant Others*; for Foxtel: *Pacific Heat*; for Network Ten: *The Secrets She Keeps*; for Seven Network: *Home and Away*; and for Showcase: *Tangle*. Lucia's film credits include *Blackrock*, *Dog*, *Look Both Ways*, *Spank*, and *Stealth*. She has won several awards including the Humanitarian of the Year Award, Oscarts Critics Best Actress and the Queen's Trust Award.

ANTHONY TAUFA

TOM RAWLINS, COACH PETER AND OTHERS

Anthony has recently finished filming the second series of *Wolf Like Me* which will air on Stan later in the year. Recently, Anthony appeared in Sydney Theatre Company's *The Tenant of Wildfell Hall* and *A Christmas Carol* for the Ensemble Theatre. Other stage credits include: for Bell Shakespeare: *The Merchant of Venice*; for Queensland Theatre: *An Octoroon*; and for Sydney Theatre Company: *A Cheery Soul*, *Cloud Nine*, *Home, I'm Darling*, *How to Rule the World*, *Saint Joan*, *Black is the New White* (Australian Tour).

ANTHONY YANGOYAN

AJ/SETH RAWLINS

Anthony was born in Sydney, Australia where he grew up in Sydney's inner west. He holds a Bachelor of Fine Arts in Acting from Victorian College of the Arts. Over the course of his career, Anthony has played a part in multiple productions including: for Griffin: *Dogged* (for which he was nominated for a Sydney Theatre Award); for ATYP: *A Clockwork Orange*; for Red Line Productions/Critical Stages: *King of Pigs*; he has also featured in *Play in a Day* for Bell Shakespeare. Other stage credits include: for Company Clan: *The Shape of Things*; and for VCA: *A View from the Bridge*, *The Cherry Orchard*, *The Comedy of Errors*, *Doctor Faustus*, *Mad Forest*. Anthony also worked on the original web series *Frank's Patch* where he played the lead role of Frank. Anthony aims to create work that promotes both inclusion and diversity within the acting industry and is passionate about working with fellow creatives to communicate meaningful and intricate stories.

ABOUT GRIFFIN

Griffin is the only theatre company in the country exclusively devoted to the development and staging of new Australian writing. Located in the historic SBW Stables Theatre, nestled in the heart of Kings Cross, Griffin has been Australia's home for the exploration of new stories since 1978.

We are the launch pad for new plays, ideas and writing that other theatres won't take a risk on. We boldly contribute to Australia's unique and powerful storytelling culture. Plays like *Prima Facie*, *Holding the Man* and *City of Gold* all had their world premieres at Griffin before going out to capture the national imagination. In the words of our longest-serving Artistic Director, **Ros Horin**:

"We are the theatre of first chances."

We are passionate about nurturing emerging and established practitioners alike. We pride ourselves on supporting our vast community of artists, audiences and supporters who consider our theatre their creative home. We help ambitious, bold, risk-taking and urgent Australian work get from the page onto the stage. We tell the stories that help us know who we are as a nation, and who we want to become.

Acknowledgement of Country

Griffin Theatre Company and the SBW Stables Theatre operate and tell stories on the unceded lands of the Gadigal of the Eora Nation. We acknowledge and honour Aboriginal and Torres Strait Islander people as the oldest continuous living culture on the planet, with more than 60,000 years of storytelling practice shaping and underpinning all aspects of Australian culture. It is a privilege that we do not take lightly: to work on this land, and to tell stories on its soil.

GRIFFIN THEATRE COMPANY
13 Craigend St
Kings Cross NSW 2011

02 9332 1052
info@griffintheatre.com.au
griffintheatre.com.au

SBW STABLES THEATRE
10 Nimrod St
Kings Cross NSW 2011

BOOKINGS
griffintheatre.com.au
02 9361 3817

GRIFFIN FAMILY

Board
Bruce Meagher (Chair)
Guillaume Babille
Nigel Barrington
Simon Burke AO
Julieanne Campbell
Lyndell Droga
Declan Greene
Nakul Legha
Julia Pincus
Lenore Robertson
Simone Whetton

Artistic Director & CEO
Declan Greene

Executive Director & CEO
Julieanne Campbell

General Manager
Khym Scott

Associate Artistic Director
Andrea James

Literary Manager
Dylan Van Den Berg

Literary Associate
Julian Larnach

Ticketing Manager
Gary Barker

Ticketing Administrator
Nathan Harrison

Production Manager
Tyler Fitzpatrick

Front of House Manager
Alex Bryant-Smith

Front of House
Riordan Berry
Kandice Joy
Max Philips
Willo Young

Head of Development
Jake Shavikin

Relationships Manager
Ell Katte

Finance Manager
Kylie Richards

Finance Consultant
Emma Murphy

Marketing Manager
Erica Penollar

Content Producer
Ang Collins

Senior Producer
Leila Enright

Administration & Ticketing Coordinator
Kate Marks

Strategic Insights Consultant
Peter O'Connell

Sustainability Coordinators
Ang Collins
Julian Larnach

Brand & Graphic Design
Alphabet

Web Developer
DevQuoll

Cover Photography
Brett Boardman

GRIFFIN DONORS

Income from Griffin activities covers less than 40% of our operating costs—leaving an ever-increasing gap for us to fill through government funding, sponsorship and the generosity of our individual supporters. Your support helps us bridge the gap and keep ticket prices affordable and our work at its best. To make a donation and a difference, contact Griffin on **9332 1052** or donate online at **griffintheatre.com.au**

PROGRAM PATRONS

Griffin Ambassadors
Robertson Foundation

Griffin Amplify
Girgensohn Foundation

Griffin Literary Manager
Robertson Foundation

Griffin Studio
Gil Appleton
Darin Cooper Foundation
Kiong Lee & Richard Funston
Ken & Lilian Horler
Malcolm Robertson Foundation
Geoff & Wendy Simpson OAM
Danielle Smith & Sean Carmody

Griffin Studio Workshop
Mary Ann Rolfe (Patron)
Iolanda Capodanno & Juergen Krufczyk
Darin Cooper Foundation
Bob & Chris Ernst
Susan MacKinnon
Pip Rath & Wayne Lonergan
Walking up the Hill Foundation

Griffin Women's Initiative
Katrina Barter
Wendy Blacklock
Jessica Block
Christy Boyce & Madeleine Beaumont
Julieanne Campbell
Iolanda Capodanno
Jane Clifford
Laura Crennan
Jennifer Darin
Lyndell Droga
Mandy Foley
Judith Fox & Yvonne Stewart
Melinda Graham
Sherry Gregory
Rosemary Hannah & Lynette Preston
Antonia Haralambis
Ann Johnson
Roanne Knox
Tessa Leong
Tory Loudon
Susan MacKinnon
Julia Pincus
Ruth Ritchie
Lenore Robertson
Deanne Weir
Simone Whetton

PRODUCTION PARTNERS 2023

As a new writing theatre, we program a wide range of stories that reflect our time, place and the unique voice of contemporary Australia. To ensure that these stories continue to be told, we need private production support for one play a year—a play that stands out in terms of its ability to articulate a new and powerful vision, that brings strength, insight and candour to the stage. Since 2015, our Production Partners have had the unique privilege of helping shape the future of Australian theatre and some of Griffin's most ambitious repertoire. It takes courage to support untried and untested work; plays that can be raw, honest and unflinching. We are so thankful for their support of Jailbaby *by* **Suzie Miller**.

Thank you:
Darin Cooper Foundation
Rachel Doyle
Lyndell & Daniel Droga
Danny Gilbert AM & Kathleen Gilbert
Rosemary Hannah & Lynette Preston
Robert Dick & Erin Shiel
Richard McHugh & Kate Morgan
Bruce Meagher & Greg Waters
Julia Pincus & Ian Learmonth
Andrew Post & Sue Quill

PRODUCTION PARTNERS 2022

***Whitefella Yella Tree* by Dylan Van Den Berg**
Lisa Barker & Don Russell
Darin Cooper Foundation
Robert Dick & Erin Shiel
Lyndell & Daniel Droga
Danny Gilbert AM & Kathleen Gilbert
Rosemary Hannah & Lynette Preston
Bruce Meagher & Greg Waters
Richard McHugh & Kate Morgan
Julia Pincus & Ian Learmonth
Pip Rath & Wayne Lonergan

SEASON DONORS

Company Patron $100,000+
Neilson Foundation

Season Patron $50,000+
Girgensohn Foundation
Robertson Foundation

Mainstage Donors $20,000+
Anonymous (1)
Darin Cooper Foundation
Robert Dick & Erin Shiel
Rosemary Hannah & Lynette Preston
Julia Pincus & Ian Learmonth
Mary Ann Rolfe

Production Donors
$10,000+
Lisa Barker & Don Russell
Rachel Doyle
Gordon & Marie Esden
Abraham & Helen James
Ingrid Kaiser
Nathan Mayfield
Richard McHugh & Kate Morgan
Bruce Meagher & Greg Waters
Tim & Sarah Minchin
Dianne & Peter O'Connell
Pip Rath & Wayne Lonergan
The WeirAnderson Foundation

Rehearsal Donors
$5,000–$9,999
Anonymous (1)
Antoinette Albert
Gil Appleton
Wendy Blacklock
Ellen Borda
Bernard Coles
Ian Dickson
Lyndell & Daniel Droga
Danny Gilbert AM & Kathleen Gilbert
Libby Higgin
Ken & Lilian Horler
Lambert Bridge Foundation
Kiong Lee & Richard Funston
Lee Lewis & Brett Boardman
Rosemary Lucas & Robert Yuen
Sophie McCarthy & Antony Green
Catriona Morgan-Hunn
Anthony Paull
Rebel Penfold-Russell OAM
Geoff & Wendy Simpson OAM
The Sky Foundation
Merilyn Sleigh & Raoul de Ferranti
Danielle Smith & Sean Carmody
Walking Up the Hill Foundation

Final Draft Donors
$3,000–$4,999
Corinne & Bryan
Bob & Chris Ernst
Jocelyn Goyen
Sherry Gregory
James Hartwright & Kerrin D'Arcy
Roanne & John Knox
Susan MacKinnon
Don & Leslie Parsonage
Leslie Stern

Workshop Donors
$1,000–$2,999
Anonymous (6)
Melissa Ball
Baly Douglass Foundation
Katrina Barter
Helen Bauer & Helen Lynch AM
Cherry & Peter Best
Jessica Block
Christy Boyce & Madeleine Beaumont
Dr Bernadette Brennan
Anne Britton
Stephen & Annabelle Burley
Iolanda Capodano & Juergen Krufczyk
Julieanne Campbell
Louise Christie
Anna Cleary
Jane Clifford
Bryony & Tim Cox
Sally Crawford
Laura Crennan
Cris Croker & David West
Ros & Paul Espie
Brian Everingham
Jan Ewert
John & Libby Fairfax
Mandy Foley
Sandra Forbes
Jennifer Giles
Nicky Gluyas
Melinda Graham
Peter Gray & Helen Thwaites
Antonia Haralambis
Kate Harrison
John Head
Mark Hopkinson & Michelle Opie
Michael Jackson
Ann Johnson
David & Adrienne Kitching
Elizabeth Laverty
Benjamin Law
Tessa Leong
Richard & Elizabeth Longes
Tory Loudon
Kyrsty Macdonald & Christopher Hazell
Prudence Manrique
Lorin Muhlmann
Ian Neuss & Penny Young
David Nguyen
Shaan Perera
Ian Phipps
Martin Portus
Annabel Ritchie
In memory of Katherine Robertson
Sylvia Rosenblum
Jann Skinner
Ann & Quinn Sloan
Geoffrey Starr
Stuart Thomas
Elizabeth Thompson
Mike Thompson
Sue Thomson
Janet Wahlquist
Richard Weinstein & Richard Benedict
Simone Whetton
Rob White & Lisa Hamilton
Rosemary White
Paul & Jennifer Winch
Elizabeth Wing

Reading Donors
$500–$999
Anonymous (3)
Brian Abel
Priscilla Adey
Jane Albert
Amity Alexander
Wendy Ashton
Robyn Ayres
Phillip Black
Claire Bornhoffen
Larry Boyd & Barbara Caine AM
Tim Capelin
Jane Christensen
Michael Diamond AM MBE
Max Dingle OAM
Elizabeth Diprose
David Earp
Leonie Flannery
Alan Froude & David Round
Peter Graves
Erica Gray
Stephanie & Andrew Harrison
David Hoskins & Paul McKnight
Sylvia Hrovatin
Nicki Jam
Mira Joksovic
Matt Jones & Rebecca Bourne Jones
Colleen Mary Kane
Susan J Kath
Patricia Lynch
Ian & Elizabeth MacDonald
Suzanne & Anthony Maple-Brown
Robert Marks
Nick Read
Chris Marrable & Kate Richardson

Simon Marrable &
Anna Kasper
Christopher Matthies
Christopher McCabe
John McCallum &
Jenny Nicholls
Daniela McMurdo
Jacqui Mercer
John Mitchell
Neville Mitchell
Keith Moynihan
Patricia Novikoff
Carolyn Penfold
Belinda Piggott &
David Ojerholm
Virginia Pursell
Alex-Oonagh Redmond
Bill Harris
Gemma Rygate
Rob & Rae Spence
Mary Stollery & Eric Dole
Catherine Sullivan &
Alexandra Bowen
Ariadne Vromen
Robyn Fortescue &
Rosie Wagstaff
Helen Wicker

First Draft Donors
$200-$499
Anonymous (11)
Susan Ambler
Elizabeth Antonievich
William Armitage
Chris Baker
Jan Barr
John Bell AO, OBE
Edwina Birch
Andrew Bowmer
Peter Brown
Wendy Buswell
Ruth Campbell
David Caulfield
Amanda Clark
Sue Clark
Louise Costanzo
Brendan Crotty &
Darryl Toohey
Bryan Cutler
Sue Donnelly
Peter Duerden
Anna Duggan
Kathy Esson
Elizabeth Evatt
Michael Eyers
Helen Ford
Judith Fox
Eva Gerber
Jock Given
Deane Golding
Keith Gow
Virginia & Kieran Greene
Jo Grisard
Edwina Guinness
Ruth Guss
Kate Haddock
Raewyn Harlock
Robert Henderson &
Marijke Conrade
Grania Hickley
Matthew Huxtable
Marian & Nabeel Ibrahim
Andrew Inglis
James Landon-Smith
Penelope Latey
Liz Locke
Danielle Long
Norman Long
Noella Lopez
Maruschka Loupis
Anni MacDougall
Claire McCaughan
Louise McDonald
Duncan McKay
Paula McLean
Stephen McNamara
Anne Miehs
Julia Mitchell
Mark Mitchell
Sarah Mort
Margaret Murphy
Carolyn Newman
Suzanne Osmond
Catherine & Joshua Palmer
Peter Pezzutti
Christopher Powell
Janelle Prescott
Andrew Pringle
Dorothy & Adit Rao
Tracey Robson
Ann Rocca
Catherine Rothery
Kevin & Shirley Ryan
Dimity Scales
Julia Selby
Natalie Shea
Vivienne Skinner
Bridget Smith
Vanda & Martin Smith
Yvonne Stewart
Augusta Supple
Danny Tomic
Rachel Trigg
Samantha Turley
Adam Van Rooijen
Julie Whitfield
Eve Wynhausen
Robert Yuen
William Zappa

We would also like to thank Peter O'Connell for his expertise, guidance and time.

CURRENT AS OF 5 JUNE 2023

GRIFFIN SPONSORS

Griffin would like to thank the following:

OUR PARTNERS

Government Supporters

Benefactor

Creative Partners

alphabet.

Company Sponsors

Griffin Theatre Company is assisted by the Australian Government through the Australia Council, its arts funding and advisory body; and the NSW Government through Create NSW.